STATE O' CHASSIS

STATE O' CHASSIS
An Earful Of Ireland

by Michael Garvey

THE THOMAS MORE PRESS
Chicago, Illinois

ISBN 0-88347-107-8

Boyle:
Chiselurs don't care a damn now about
their parents, they're bringin' their fathers' grey hairs down with sorra to the
grave, an' laughin' at it, laughin' at it. Ah,
I suppose it's just the same everywhere—
the whole worl's in a state o' chassis.

Juno and the Paycock
by Sean O'Casey

INTRODUCTION

A good friend of mine has a particular weakness for generalization. He'll tell you, without blushing, that there were no unemployed midgets during the Second World War; that thunder has never been heard in Cuba; that Italians are capable of developing ulcers. Most of his beliefs are difficult to dispute, since it's difficult to find the unemployed midget, the startled Cuban, or the belching Italian needed for contradictory evidence. One time, sober and unblinking, my friend told me that the literary community of Ireland had never produced an honest book review, and I thought I had him.

When I questioned him about this remarkable assertion, he explained that Ireland's critical dishonesty was a consequence of the island's claustrophobic size and societal intricacy. Although I'm not sure I agree with him, I think his reasoning is cogent. Let me explain.

As a native of the North American continent, I may boldly and publicly denounce the writing of Norman Mailer, or even his character. I could insist to anyone idle enough to listen that Norman Mailer is about as tough as a boiled Twinkie and that I could beat him Indian-wrestling. In the unusual circumstance

that Norman Mailer got wind of and cared
about my accusation, he would have to search
fifty states from the rocky Maine headlands to
Hawaii's tropic shores to give me a black eye.
But if I lived, say, in Dingle, Co. Kerry, and
Mr. Mailer lived in Muff, Co. Donegal, only a
few hours scenic driving would prevent him
from registering his disagreement with me.
Morever, my publisher would be a friend or
relative of Norman Mailer; he would refuse to
publish my remarks or pay me shockingly less
money for them. (My real, unimagined publisher, come to think of it, hasn't exactly made a
millionaire out of me.) I could not drink in a
Dublin pub free from the fear that I could turn
from my pint to behold an enraged, aging, and
highly-skilled boxer who'd heard I thought he
was yellow; some evil-minded relative might
invite me to a party which Mailer was sure to
attend. And so on.

In thanking the many Irish people who were
so unreasonably good to me during my too-
brief visit, I confront a problem much like the
one my generalizing friend has observed, or
imagined. Anyone I thank here would know at
least two other kind people I've neglected to
mention, and to whom I owe deep gratitude.
However, I wish especially to thank St. Patrick
(if he won't mind representing clergymen),

Cathleen Ni Hoolihan (who certainly won't mind representing Irishwomen), and Finn McCool (the greatest representative of Irishmen). There was one man who identified himself as a member of the Special Branch of the Gardai in Dublin who was a real jerk. I wish not to thank him at all.

I should also emphasize that these thanks precede the observations of one twenty-seven year old Northamerican male, and may (unfortunately) provide much more information about twenty-seven year old Northamerican males than about the world's most triumphantly unexplainable country. Among the citizenry of a nation where the number of dead crows along the roadside is an explosive issue, the confused observations of a foreigner's visit are going to annoy somebody; I'd be offended if they didn't. In any case, there is no harm intended, except to the bishops, who won't read this.

Any of my Irish friends who are, for whatever reason, offended, I now invite to stay at my house in Davenport, Iowa, where they may write reciprocally inaccurate reports about me.

PROFOUND mistrust of technology, that was the thing. Having given it a name, I was reassured and thus my exuberant spirit (I was going to Ireland!) was rescued from its sweaty, tachycardiac nose-dive. The whole thing had been triggered by a word, too.

There I was, three or four miles above the waters of the North Atlantic, happily sipping bourbon and flirting with a beautiful English woman. She said that Ireland was lovely. And Ireland, she said, was "authentic".

I started to go crazy. Authenticity-lust was a loony catalyst for this journey. Hurtling through the North Atlantic sky, powered by Arabian fuel, the occupants of an aluminum tube were sipping liquids distilled from Kentucky grains, rattling frozen Lake Michigan water in small translucent containers made out of petroleum from Texas. In a few minutes, the inside of the tube would be plunged into darkness and a broomstick-width beam of silver light would issue from a whirring box. The images projected by the beam would lull the tube's occupants into a stupor by imitating the sexual fantasies of a Los Angeles capitalist. We were going to that green, wet land where imagination and material were more chaste in their dealings with each other. Folly, there, would not be satanic, but impish. I settled back into my seat.

The perversity of a travel agent obligated my first (and, please God, my only) experience of Heathrow airport. A grumpy, spaced-out transatlantic passenger whose misfortune it is to touch down at Heathrow must immediately encounter the world's most unyielding security measures. These might be reasonable if they weren't gratuitous.

Let's say I'm a terrorist, my thoughts ran as a Pakastani guard dismantled the portable radio my brother wanted me to take to a friend, and I want to plunge Heathrow into complete chaos. The job would be done before I arrived there. But let's say I wanted to hit Pat Boone in the face with a chocolate pudding pie, taking him by surprise as he waited for a plane.

In the very unlikely event that anyone knew where his plane was boarding, I'd have to take a bus to get there, and the bus, if I could find it (since nobody seems to know where the buses board either), would remain immobile for half an hour, when a smiling, turban-topped man who could speak no English would drive it through the dangerous inner labyrinth of the place, depositing me two miles from any recognizable airport building. By the time I could arrive at Pat Boone's gate, his plane would have left, or mine would have, or I'd have grown hungry and eaten the pie. Obviously the place to hit Pat Boone is O'Hare.

The Pakistani's explorations soon satisfied him that my brother's radio contained no explosives; new frenzies were unleashed. Frisked, spun, questioned, stamped, encouraged, welcomed to Great Britain (at one point, I think, inoculated) and asked how long I intended to stay in Zambia, I gritted my teeth and muttered "Ireland" over and over again, as if the name were my mantra. A sympathetic Briton shoved me onto a crowded bus.

The rest of the airport delirium was too relentless and painful to describe, ending, after what seemed miles of Heathrow white water, in a more subdued eddy around a green sign which read Aer Lingus-Shannon. Frail and numb, suspecting still that this was another airport mirage, I collapsed into a vinyl chair, stumbling over the extended boots of an unconscious cowboy opposite me. He had been snoring into the amplifying hollow of the ten gallon hat which shielded his face from the flourescent light, but my clumsiness woke him, and he sat up quickly, alert and suspicious:

"Ireland?" he snapped.

"I think so." He seemed relieved.

"Good. I think so, too." I was relieved that somebody else thought so. We stared around uneasily, until the cowboy spoke again. "This," he said solemnly, "is the fifth *goddamned* time I've been through this *goddamned* place this *goddamned* week."

"Is it always this nuts?"

"You're goddamn right, son. Goddamn worse yesterday."

"You travel a lot?"

"Too goddamn much, if ya ask me. Sometimes I forget where I live."

After this much Heathrow, I wasn't sure where I lived either; it was good to meet someone else who realized that this was a bad place, and the cowboy and I started to talk. He was from Lubbock, Texas, and in the construction business with a brother-in-law. Apparently, their business had metastasized frighteningly, flinging startled Texans into the deserts of the Persian Gulf, the jungles of the Nile Basin, and the summits of New Zealand Alps. The cowboy hated travel, but must carry a passport stamped by customs officials of every U.N. government; his present intention (aside from the unattainable dream of returning to Lubbock, where ready-mix concrete was made available by a single phone call) was to spend two nights at a Shannon Airport hotel in the arms of his girl friend, an Aer Lingus employee. I argued with him about his lack of interest in what anyone else would consider a dazzling nomadic existence, but he insisted that if only I visited Lubbock I would understand. What would the Irish make of this nut?

What would they make of me?

Disembarking at Shannon Airport was, if much gentler than the turbulent experience of Heathrow, equally bewildering. Expecting close, grey, wet weather, we found Limerick harsh and glittering with intense sunlight; unchallenged, we went hesitantly along complicated and empty corridors, and the bigness of the place seemed to swallow up the Heathrow passengers. Suddenly, as if the event were part of a dream, I found myself in a large white barren room facing a uniformed man who seemed startled by my entrance. Afraid that I'd taken a wrong turn someplace, I asked, "Is this customs?"

"It is." At first I thought I'd been too blunt; the customs official seemed almost embarrassed by the question and unsure what to do or say next. We stood there uncomfortably, avoiding each other's eyes, as if the institution of a border were a painful, intimate thing to be confronted with delicacy and charity. But I was sick of airports and badly wanted to be

15

outdoors in the uncharacteristically sunny
countryside.
"Well, then. What next?"
"Ah. Yes. Next. Well. Em." The official
seemed to have been disgorged from a day-
dream. He coughed, shifted on his feet and
became suddenly serious. "These are your
things, are they?"
"Yes."
"Well, then. Personal stuff, I suppose, too."
"Yes."
"Well. And this is all you have with you, is
it?"
"That's it."
"Grand." Silence again, and again he
looked awkward.
"Well, then, can I go?"
"Oh! Yes you may, surely. Welcome to Ireland." His reluctance to be businesslike,
especially after the excruciating thoroughness
of the Heathrow staff, was a potent delight.
Overjoyed, I rushed through the terminal into
the alien sunshine.

I think I was looking for a revolution. Americans, especially young ones, are always looking for revolutions, probably because our own
so dramatically hit the skids in the late 1960's.
It was a feeble, pathetic little revolution all
right, probably doomed from the start, origi-

nating, as it did, in an opulent country where fantasy and reality never were forced too far apart. But we tried.

Taking into account the widespread and intense lunacy of the sixties, William Irwin Thompson's identification of American student radicals as "the peasants of our technological society . . . disfiguring the monuments and attacking the ceremonial centers" was justified. As a teenager visiting Boston when the first news of the Kent State killings transpired, I remember an impressively well-attended rally at which an angry Maoist orator (who probably now is a cost systems analyst for E.F. Hutton) urged his listeners to delay the revolution no further; "The Pigs have declared war on you!" His rancor was stirring, and reflected the widespread, inarticulable notion that somehow, all of us were being used. By "them". Cambridge was like a clenched fist, and the children of stockbrokers and corporate lawyers tossed months of spending-money into the Che Guevera berets which circulated in their gathering. This was America, where money was energy, where the Pigs had declared war. Assiduously encouraging us, San Francisco Mime Troupe members carried the berets, assuring that each nickel would buy a bullet for one of "them". Misdirected and febrile as those passions were, it still is aston-

ishing that such white-hot madness could have
so little lasting effect. What seems in retrospect an adolescent tantrum seemed then a
historical convulsion. Forced now to acknow-
ledge the transition of that enraged roar to a
petulant whine (accomplished by that Confu-
cian genius who ended involuntary conscrip-
tion) we are naturally jaded and cynical. We
thought then that the world must change.
    (And it did change. "They" won, and "they"
in fact grew exponentially more powerful.
"They" will soon deploy twenty-seven Trident
submarines, any one of which could vaporize
the major population-centers of an entire
hemisphere, so to hell with "them". That's
their purpose, methodology, and ultimate destination. The search for any alternative is
urgent; rumors of any significant change are
immediately intoxicating.)
    Friends of mine, even some Irish friends,
had told me that there was a revolution going
on in Ireland. True, Ireland had almost institu-
tionalized revolution, as anyone who ever
heard a middle-aged, undersexed South Boston
drunk praising the Provisional IRA knows; but
this one was different. It was more than romantic Clancy Brother songs and fond memor-
ies of 1916; it was simply a momentous change
of a social circumstance: Young people were
staying in Ireland.

State O'Chassis

Something had to be going on.

The bus-route between the airport and the city of Limerick, from which I'd decided to hitchhike southwest, was disquieting, and depressing signs of American hegemony were pronounced along the road. A billboard advertising Guinness Stout underlined a depiction of three dew-spangled pints with the slogan, "Black is Beautiful"; newly pubescent children, collected at the many bus-stops, wore John Travolta T-shirts; Star Wars posters dotted the telephone poles and gas stations boasted "genuine American ice cream." Colonel Sanders' had even arrived in Limerick, and although he was smiling benignly from above his restaurant (the duplicate of the one in Fargo, North Dakota), I thought there was something leering and evil in that face. If young people were staying in Ireland, their American cousins wanted a piece of the meat.

The bus stopped beside the chicken place and began to empty. Still weakened by the transatlantic delirium, I was alarmed by the Colonel's stare. Like the face of Burl Ives in *Cat on a Hot Tin Roof*, it seemed carnal and vicious, the face of a despotic southern patriarch come to conquer Limerick. I was blocking the exit.

"Move it, will ye? Yer holdin' up the whole

foogin' production!" The angry shout and shove jolted me from the bus, and, sheepish, I turned to see the inconvenienced passenger. Sr. Mary Alverna, my eighth grade teacher, would have called him "a juvenile delinquent". In my state, I couldn't have called him anything at all, unable to do anything but stare dumbly at him as he glared and flashed that gesture which in the American sixties meant Peace and which, in the British Isles means something else. As he dramatized his understandable annoyance, I noticed a tattoo on his right forearm. It was a garish green dagger with a serpent curled around the hilt. On the blade was inscribed one word: Erin. A terrible beauty indeed.

In the century that seemed to elapse between that encounter and my first ride (or "lift", as the Irish hitchhikers with whom I competed said), I walked three or four miles from the Limerick outskirts. Thronged on both sides by new and often half-built houses, each glittering in the weird sunlight, the road seemed itself a symptom of change. Antiquated, preconceived (and probably condescending) notions of "authentic" Ireland were quickly evaporating in my flight-addled brain; I was as unprepared for the tropical temperature as for the large infusions of money betokened by the omnipresent evidence of housing-boom. The surrealism intensified with the first lift: a carload of German university students.

They seemed at first disappointed that I was not a local, a fact which was quickly established when the driver, who spoke the best English in the group, pointed to a roadsign and asked me to pronounce a word that looked like Arvggh. But they were friendly, anyway, and we passed the next half-hour telling cryptic ethnic jokes about the inhabitants of some Bavarian region. My German is as extensive as my Protohittite, which meant that many of the punchlines became garbled: "Why iss a fellow frum Verschbyrt not alvays in trouble? Because to him dun't come de (the German-English dictionary would be produced then) . . . fracht thinks? No . . . " I was as impatient as they were by the time they turned off the main road, leaving me astounded in the transformed Irish countryside.

As the effects of jetlag began to diminish, the irritation of being passed by dozens of smiling, apologetically shrugging motorists (always in otherwise empty cars) increased. I improvised what I thought was a pretty convincing limp, but by the time I'd perfected this device, the road had become deserted.

There was a distant, wailing sound first, haunting as a mile-off freight train, and then a striking, familiar, nasal whine. I thought I was hallucinating as a consequence of the heat, or the prolonged sleeplessness; but I heard the music even before the drone of the approaching engine. By the time the car had pulled off to my side of the road, ten yards past me, the blare was unmistakable, a thing I'd heard on afternoons hotter than this one, in the house where I grew up, even years before Sr. Alverna had warned our eighth grade class about juvenile delinquents. It was the music of Bob Dylan, and the words of "Oxford Town", emitted from the small cassette-player, seemed as inappropriate and out of place as everything else in this strange day. The smiling driver hopped out of the car and flopped back the front seat. I thanked him for stopping, stepped over one of the jerry-rigged cassette speakers, and found myself next to an overweight, bespectacled, earth goddess in a small backseat compartment reeking of potsmoke. "I'm Starwoman," she said in a Cork accent as broad and complex as the history of Ireland.

I'd made contact with the guerrillas.

Starwoman and her two male companions were mirthfully wrecked, and full of questions about America. Her very name amazed me, sounding, as it did, like a late-sixties Haight-Ashbury export, but by now, even after so

short a time in a foreign land, it took a con-
scious effort to be amazed. The unexpected
conditions over here made it seem logical to be
driving through the brilliant countryside with
refugees (Irish-accented refugees) from a Jack
Kerouac novel, chatting about the subculture
as Dylan sang songs about racial war and as-
sassinations of civil rights leaders. The driver
was meticulous; cheerfully inclining his head
towards the back seat, he kept describing the
whole event with the word "wow", but never
took his eyes off the road. Next to him, a blond,
afro-haired, smiling but silent hippie tinkered
with the bass and treble controls of the tape-
recorder. Aside from the wowing driver, Starwoman did most of the talking. She swore she'd
never been in America, but whenever I asked
her questions about Ireland, her replies, probably as an effect of the grass, grew complicated and opaque.

I was learning very little about Ireland.
Well, I was fast learning that I knew far less
than I thought I knew about it, but I was beginning to learn as well what had happened to a
recently antique American style, and I was
trying to fight off the pang of condescension
emerging in the wake of the discovery.

All those dark enthusiasms and loony passions stirred up by our American adolescent

revolt had turned mellow before they died. All that energy, all that spirit, all that pot . . . what happened to those things? American poetry enjoyed "the San Francisco Rennaisance", the Grateful Dead began to record lovely music, and Woodstock drew a larger crowd than Superbowl XIII. Nobody who was American, young, and bourgeois will ever forget that pleasant time. But what happened to all that?

It ran out of steam, and I learned this afternoon, it fled to a green and dreamy land.

State O'Chassis

*T*HANK GOD that in our tradition a priest's intelligence and personality have only marginally to do with his divine calling. The office transcends the man, we were told as children, and if we did not cling to this truth, our numbers in the world would be considerably reduced. Ireland, perhaps the most fervently Catholic country in the West, is a working illustration of this wisdom. I can honestly say that I've never heard an Irish priest say anything worth listening to (at least from the pulpit), but this may not be their fault.

Many virtuous and otherwise charming people are sporadically susceptible to the belief that no matter how long they talk, what they have to say is important. Civilization, with its whiskey, coffee, and amphetamines makes the most holy of us vulnerable to this illusion. To provide for the defect, God sends most of us friends, spouses and sometimes even strangers to tell us that we're boring. Divine agents who tell us to shut up. Increasingly, this phenomenon is looked upon as a compelling argument in favor of married clergy, and the reasoning is attractive. Marriage could provide an emotional space—impossible in the solitude of a rectory—in which the sensitive clerical spouse could amputate the redundancies of the average Sunday homily. Angry laypeople can't tell a priest that he's boring them, and that the ministry of the Gospel is being made sluggish by superfluous verbal weight. (Well, they could tell him, but he wouldn't listen.) But if the priest were, like any sane man, frightened of his wife, she could.

Of course, the best rebuttal here is a comparison of Fulton Sheen and Billy Graham. If Fulton Sheen were married and Billy Graham were celibate, most people would agree that neither would be any less boring. Another solution will have to be found.

But why, in verbal, Catholic Ireland, is an interesting sermon as rare as a snake, a wolf, or an operable pay phone? Human history does, after all, occasionally yield people who can speak for hours about things which, if not always of earthshaking importance, are interesting. Peter Maurin, for example, who was known to speak for periods of up to twelve hours in length, was never assassinated and died peacefully. In Bourbonaisse, Illinois, there is a housewife who can expand an ordinary declarative sentence into a lucid, but baroque grammatical symphony capable of holding the most jaded or impatient listener spellbound for an entire afternoon. And although this is an unusual gift, it is bestowed more frequently and generously on the people of Ireland—as literature, cliche, and sometimes uncharitable ridicule all attest—than on any other people in the world. Revolting as the hackneyed concept of "blarney" is to anyone who loves the country as I do, it is grounded more in objective scrutiny than in prejudice. These folks can talk. And talk.

So my sorrow when I heard in Derry that Pope Paul VI had finally met with the death which he seemed to long for was twofold: (1) A good, holy, and misunderstood man had died at the helm of the Church whose confusion and turmoil greatly saddened him; (2) I, hearing of his passing, was absent from the Granby Bar, whose patrons are, in my opinion, among the greatest talkers in Ireland. At such a jarring existential moment, as at a birth, a marriage, the death of a loved one, or a Notre Dame-Southern Cal game, the urge to surround oneself with a particular cluster of people overrides everything else. When I imagined the things being said about Pope Paul and his Church at the Granby Bar, the verbal terrain of the Bogside became, in contrast, as barren as the surface of Mars and as monotonous as the long sermon on the Transfiguration, of all things, to which I, with hundreds of other

Catholics had been subjected that morning. I had to go to Dublin.

But it was three days before I could return to the Free State from the Six Counties. When, finally, I found myself impatient and distracted on the Belfast-Dublin train, having read the *Independent* three times, I pacified myself for awhile by trying to remember the name of the Charles Bronson movie in which an escape from a Mexican jail was achieved by the use of a helicopter (there was a reason for this, and I'll explain later). I narrowed the possibilities down to "Breakout" and "Escape," both of which were probably miles off, and at last decided to abandon the project. It may seem strange that a passenger on a long train ride through some of the most beautiful country in the Western World could be reduced to these efforts, but the tall hedges which invariably obscure the view from railroad tracks in Ireland present to the passenger's eye little more than a perforated green blur. The visual atmosphere is not much different from that of Nebraska. To keep my sanity, I pretended to sleep and, behind closed eyes, reflected on my first experience at the Granby Bar.

Only a romantic, or perhaps a drunk, would tell you that there is no such thing as a generation gap in Ireland. In Ireland, as all over the

West, teenagers are, for the most part, loud, rude and unpleasant. There, as everywhere else, older folk find the appearance, music and values of the new generation repulsive. The heresy of youth worship flourishes in Ireland as in America, the countries of the European Economic Community, or any capitalist country where the demands of expanding markets require that simple people be brainwashed into believing that expensive products will make them young or immortal. But perhaps through the institution of the public house, aided by the grace of God, a benign neglect of the wide generation gap is a cultural circumstance peculiar to Ireland. A feminist would be displeased by the predominance of male interests and patronage in Irish pubs, but almost anyone would be gratified by the ease and grace with which young and old seem to mix there. Old men and young men converse and buy rounds without a hint of condescension or mockery, and beneath a haze of Guinness and whiskey you can see the peaceful interaction of age groups, as if they didn't instinctively mistrust and despise each other. It is a pleasing contradiction which will never be satisfactorily explained. It is exemplified by the patrons of the Granby Bar.

The Granby Bar could be described as a

typical Dublin pub, if such a thing exists. Standing with your back to the bar, which you would never do, since such a posture would make you immediately and uncomfortably conspicuous, you would face a row of half a dozen small round tables fronting a black upholstered shelf. Perched on the shelf, and arranged in a series of human tryptics would be the Granby's clientele. Pint glasses and whiskey glasses would forest the table before each group and the flow of words would be impressive. With very few exceptions, each group would consist of a very old man doing most of the talking, a much younger man doing less, and a third man of any age at all doing nothing but nodding now and then. At those rare times when a conversation stalled or needed refueling, this usually silent Dubliner would contribute a vague affirmative or politely interrogative noise. I've imitated this noise for people in Iowa, and they all claim to find it convincingly accurate, but I suspect that it cannot be accurately reproduced by anyone whose family has ever left Ireland. It is made by an intricate harmony of the larynx and the windpipe, a sharp, throaty inhalation, and it is generally used as a connective. (In certain contexts, it could translate into "I know," "you're right," "how true," "isn't it," or "uh huh.") It has been used in Gaelic and in English, I'm certain, since pre-Patrician times, and gives to the most mundane conversation intensity and robust cadence.

On my first visit to the Granby Bar, "the noise" was used by a guy about my age in response to my admission that I was American. Having confirmed my nationality, he asked me if I'd like to buy a gram of hashish. I declined, explaining my poverty and ignorance of Irish law, and rambling on about my personal tastes, fears of international incidents, and astonishment that anyone could be crazy enough to approach a perfect stranger (who might, after all, be an Interpol agent) with an illegal product. Thoroughly impressed with my own eloquence, I watched for his reaction, and was disappointed when all he did was shake his head as if in exasperated pity.

"Ye don't realize what yer missin', man," he said sadly, " 'tis Vietnamese and the very best."

"I'd always heard that Australian hash was the finest." (This may or may not be true. I don't even know whether any hash is produced in Australia, but the idea seemed exotic and consequently good for a chat.)

"I wouldn't say so at all. Vietnamese is yer only man."

"I *have* heard that Vietnamese marijuana is more potent than other kinds."

The salesman looked triumphant, as if I'd just proven his point. "Well, then, there ye are. Were ye never in the army there?"

"No. I was a conscientious objector then."

"A pacifist, is it?"

"Yes." The hash salesman inhaled sharply, implying that it was a grand thing to be a pacifist, or implying that no one of sound mind could be a pacifist, or implying that he was, or had once known, a pacifist. Probably implying nothing at all. During the ambivalent silence which followed this implication, I glanced to my left and noticed an old man who seemed to have been listening to our conversation. Leaning against the bar with his cap pulled down to his eyebrows, he massaged one temple with the fingers of his left hand tucked under the brim, looking at us with such fierce interest that I thought he was angry about something. The attempted dope sale, perhaps. The presence of a pacifist, perhaps. Both, perhaps.

The salesman spoke to him first. "Ye're lookin' well, Joe."

Joe said nothing, and continued to stare. We waited.

Joe said: "Vi-et-nam," punching each syllable as if the word contained the recorded history of the Orient.

We waited a little longer, and he said it
again. Leaning forward, the salesman
watched Joe carefully.

"I suppose," Joe began, sounding like a confident poker player raising a bet, "that each
one of the two of ye are familiar with the fella
by the name of Ho-Chi-Minh?" Oh boy. The
salesman and I looked at each other, nodded,
and looked back to Joe, agreeing that we'd
heard the name before.

"Well, now, I wouldn't expect either of ye to
believe what I'm about to tell ye. Ye could say
'Joe's drunk' er 'Joe's mad' er 'Joe's a bloody
eejit' and I wouldn't care at all what ye were
sayin' but . . . " Joe paused for such a long time
that it seemed he considered the story finished. Suddenly he spoke again, his voice lowered and confidential, "Yer man and myself
were the best of friends." Obviously aware
that he had now our full attention, Joe stared
for a long time into his pint as if he were trying
to decide the proper approach to this ungainly
story. During this hesitation, it occurred to me
that Joe, the salesman, and I were forming
another one of the Granby tableaux; I felt a
grin crossing my face, which I couldn't reor-
ganize in time. Joe looked up sharply. "Ye don't
believe me." It was an accusation.

The salesman defended me. "He does, I'd
say. The story, Joe."

Reiterating his indifference to our asessment of it, Joe began the telling of the most incredible story I've ever heard. How he and Ho had been porters at the Gresham Hotel, Ho being at the time an impoverished and itinerant student. About the long and enjoyable talks they'd had in this very pub. Ho and Joe, the most feared and revered drinking team in Dublin, barred from every public house save this one here. Ho, enraged over the unfairness of Gresham wages; Joe, dutifully upholding Western apologetics, explaining to the Vietnamese the evils of atheistic communism. Ho's painful decision to leave Dublin, the city of which he was so fond; Joe's remonstration; Ho's insistence; their mutual vow of loyalty transcending geography, creed, culture, and political bent.

The salesman left for the Gents while Ho and Joe were arguing about the virtues and defects of Ireland, and did not return until the two were saying goodbye on the steps of Ho's Corkbound train. The story seemed finished, and I adjourned for the Gents myself.

When I returned, an awful lot had happened, and the story had risen to a more grandiose plateau. While I had been in the Gents, Joe had enlisted (for reasons I could never find out) in the British army. In some war and in some way, he had been captured by French soldiers, who had, somehow, decided that his talents could be put to profitable use in the staff officers' mess. What Joe didn't already know about cooking he bluffed until he finished reading an Escoffier mysteriously obtained at some moment of his internment, and he found himself cooking highly praised meals for French officers at Dien Bien Phu, of all places. "I suppose," said Joe, taking a momentary break from the story, "that ye're both familiar with Dien-Bien-Phu." Proud of my vast historical knowledge, I immediately assured Joe that I was, but the salesman, irreverently disregarding the climax towards which Joe's story was obviously building, chose this moment to ask Joe if he'd ever sampled the hashish in the region. Annoyed, Joe dismissed the question by saying that in his day, he'd tried and done several things which would astonish the salesman, myself, and anyone else for all that. The story which now engulfed the three of us, was simply another incident in an exhausting life.

Well, Dien Bien Phu, after the long and bloody siege, fell to the Vietnamese, and you'll never guess who "rode into the French camp on a white horse to dictate the terms and accept the surrender." And who recognized Joe, standing among the French prisoners. And all the rest.

At closing time, the salesman left to sample

some of his own hash, and Joe and Ho were still drinking together at Dien Bien Phu. I had to get some sleep, so I returned to my bed-and-break-fast; I'll probably never know how Joe returned to the Granby.

My eyes were still closed tightly and Joe's balloon flight of a story was vanishing among the phosphenes as the train pulled into Connolly Station. About an hour later, I stood before the locked door of the Granby. It was the Holy Hour, and for sixty minutes the doors of every Dublin pub would be closed, admitting no one but random, inquisitive policemen. If you are in a bar when Holy Hour begins, you are asked to step away from the windows and keep quiet. Whiskey and porter are still bought and sold, but in a more pensive, hushed atmosphere. There is a hint of guilt in the air and a mild sense of getting away with something. Most people will tell you that the reason for Holy Hour is the barmen's union, which insists that this is the only time a barman can eat lunch. Behind the closed doors, though, the activity of the barmen seems no less gruelling and frantic, and if you persist in questioning the practicality of the institution, most Dubliners will retort: You Yanks have all the answers, haven't you? The indignation is understand-

able; mysteries such as these are the under-
pinnings of a fascinating urban culture, and to
challenge them is not only pointless, but impolite.

Congratulating myself for my courtesy, I
passed the door of the Granby without trying
the latch or knocking. I would spend Holy Hour
investigating the truth of a rumor I'd heard,
that Oliver Plunkett was interred at the Pro
Cathedral, not far away.

Before I could make it to the Pro Cathedral, a
soft, steady rain had begun to fall and the air
was thick with the explosions of opening um-
brellas. In ten seconds every available square
inch of eye-ball level space was filled with an
umbrella-top, obliging me to make my approach to the shelter of the Cathedral porch in
a defensive crouch. At last confident that I
could straighten up without fear of eye injury, I
assumed normal posture and was delighted to
find myself face to face with Mary, a retarded
beggar whom I'd met three weeks ago in front
of the G.P.O. Whether or not she recognized
me, I'm not sure, but her face brightened, and
she refused to accept the 10p coin which I nervously tried to drop into her cigar box; it could
be that my remembering her name made us
friends, elevating our relationship beyond the
customary beggar-pedestrian class.

Her reply, when I asked what she was doing away from O'Connell Street, was a pleasant, but incomprehensible mixture of thick Dublin accent and speech impediment; still, it gave the impression that she'd been moved along by one of the Dublin guards, and even as she spoke, she glanced to her left where a guard leaned against a pillar, apparently oblivious to both of us.

To anyone who lives or spends a lot of time in Dublin, I'm sure that Mary is a familiar figure. In marked contrast to the rest of her dress, which is typically ragged and worn, she wears an elaborately knit, multi-colored shawl. This could be a calculated asset to her method of survival, because it makes her difficult to ignore, a quality which, for obvious reasons, is essential to a beggar. But without her shawl, Mary would be striking and attractive, with her curly brown hair, oval pale face, and stunning blue eyes. She retains, even in her poverty, and in her awkward connection with the rest of Dublin's society, a dignity, cheerfulness, and grace beside which the average Madonna would look like a hag. If Fellini were making a movie about Mary, he'd probably want Faye Dunnaway to play the part. (Hell, Fellini might want Patty Duke, for that matter, or Phyllis Diller, or Telly Savalas, or even

Mary Tyler Moore. Whoever he wanted, he would try to make Mary a symbol of one thing or another, which would ruin the depiction. Mary is that remarkable thing, a beggar with dignity and self-esteem, as individual as a snowflake.)

Many of Dublin's beggars are obnoxious and rudely persistent, but it's easy to see why. As is the case in most cities, more affluent pedestrians tend, with corresponding rudeness, to ignore them, escalating the ugliness of the whole situation. "Give not to me, if ye like," an old beggar woman told a friend of mine, "but don't ignore me." My friend, a priest, sometimes argues with beggars, but at least he treats them with the same fraternal hostility with which he would treat me if I were bothering him.

Standing with Mary on O'Connell Street when we first met, I found myself infuriated with the way she was treated by the many priests she encountered. They were, for the most part, considerate, polite and generous, and my instinctive anticlericalism was, as a result, uncomfortably challenged.

But there they were, the turkeys, pouring 10p coins into Mary's cigar box, even stopping a few minutes to exchange pleasantries with her, demolishing my carefully constructed theories about the moral sterility of the Irish clergy. Could it be that only in liturgical or parochial surroundings, rudeness became a charism of Holy Orders? Defensively, I savoured the memory of the Kerry priest who interrupted the Canon of the Mass, confronting the large numbers who pressed forward prematurely to the communion rail. It was as if he had been personally offended: "I would remind you that we do *not* come forward to Communion until we have said 'Oh Lord, I am not worthy . . .' " None of the people, may God be good to them, paid any attention, and the communion rail was packed by the time he had finished his silly tirade. I'll bet that the priest has been repeating this chastisement at every Mass for the last ten years, and that he has been totally ignored each time. Yet another mystery.

Mary and I chatted for awhile on the steps, occasionally pausing as she offered her cigar box to arriving and departing worshipers. To the ones who stopped and gave her a coin, she smiled and made a garbled sound like "thanks"; to the ones who hurried past, making the sign of the cross and averting their eyes, she smiled and shrugged. She continued to be nervous about the nearby guard, although he continued to take no notice of us; deciding that she was probably bothered as well by the fact that our conversation could draw his attention, I excused myself and approached the cop to ask him about Oliver Plunkett.

"Is Oliver Plunkett buried in there?"

The guard looked startled and seemed reluctant to speak. It could be that all Dublin cops are required to attend seminaries for Aloofness Training. Always polite, always helpful, usually competent, they all seem to approach verbal exchange as if each syllable were a potential bribe. Perhaps I would be shy if I were a Dublin guard. They're an unarmed force and so must depend (much as the visible Church must depend) upon the maintenance of a mysterious, slightly menacing aura for their survival. In some sections of Dublin, guards have been pulled from their cars and beaten up, a possibility which, I'm sure, contributes heavily to their apparent desire to reduce social interaction to essentials. He coughed.

"Please?"

"Oliver Plunkett. The saint. Can you tell me if he's buried here?"

"I'm sorry, I can't. Inquire inside." He was gone. His tone had implied that he *knew* where Oliver Plunkett was buried, but that police regulations would not allow him to dispense this information. Mary, at any rate, seemed re-

Michael Garvey

lieved that he was gone. Smiling, she made another garbled noise. It sounded like "Woda", and not understanding, I agreed and went into the church.

Wall to wall old ladies, and not a Mass in sight. Historians and sociologists give lists of reasons for the failure of the Reformation in Ireland, but I'm convinced that among the principal difficulties with which the anti-Papists were confronted, was the old lady problem. The English didn't know what to do with all the old ladies. Cromwell tried murdering them, but he was understaffed. For six weeks and in a dozen Irish counties, I searched for a Catholic Church containing less than ten old ladies and could find none. Protestant churches in Ireland are usually devoid of old ladies, or of any human beings, but this is probably because most of them, like most American Catholic churches, are locked when no services are going on.

In the Cathedral information office, beneath a poster advertising a travel package for Lourdes, there was a large portrait of Pope Paul, encircled, of course, in black crepe. An old lady stood in front of the picture, smiling and stroking the frame, as if it were the cheek of a child.

"That dear, dear, sweet man," she was saying. "He was in heaven days ago, I'm sure. We've no need to let him get between us and our sleep, have we?" She probably hadn't slept since his death, but I agreed that we had no need at all. Did I, she asked, want to know what time the televised Memorial Mass for Pope Paul would be celebrated? I was more interested in Oliver Plunkett's tomb; could she tell me if it was in the Pro Cathedral? All sorts of dignitaries would be at the Mass, she said, as if I should reconsider. That was wonderful, I agreed, and hadn't Dr. O'Fiach gone to Rome for the funeral, too? He had, she thought. Did she know where Oliver Plunkett was buried? The Taoseach might be there as well, she said, if he hasn't left for Rome with the Primate, and the crowds would be so large that I'd have to be there at least an hour early if I wanted a seat. All right, what time was the Memorial Mass? She told me; I think it was 8:30. Now could she tell me if Oliver Plunkett's tomb was here? She was sorry, she said, but it wasn't in Dublin at all (as if she would have been happy to move it for me if only I'd given her enough notice) but in Drogheda, she thought; I should make sure that I was here an hour early. I thanked her and left her with Pope Paul.

Drogheda. Was that what Mary had meant by Woda? She had disappeared from the Cathedral porch, but the guard was back. As I passed him, I said, "It's in Drogheda."
He touched the brim of his cap. "Sir?"
"Plunkett's tomb. In case anyone else asks you."
Then the guard made the longest speech I've ever heard made by a Dublin cop: "Matt Talbot. Will he do? Quite close to here."
Matt Talbot would not do. Holy Hour was over, and I headed for the Granby.
The commingling of the sacred and the secular realms is an ancient Irish tradition. Patrick's interaction with the Druids would have been less harmonious were it not for Christianity's peculiar genius in grafting itself on to local custom and everyday life. The results can be seen almost anywhere in Ireland. In Dublin Airport, prominently marked ticket booths are set aside for Lourdes' pilgrims. Near the site of the Old Nelson Pillar, on O'Connell Street, a statue of the Blessed Virgin keeps an eye on crossing pedestrians and cursing bus drivers. In the broadcasting schedule of RTE, the Irish television network, there are pauses at noon and at six for the chimes of the Angelus Bell. The most valuable player of a Gaelic football match is photographed as he genuflects to

kiss the ring of an overweight bishop. (It was only a few years ago, someone told me, that the crowds attending the All Ireland Final, would stand before the match to sing, "Faith of Our Fathers".)

The Granby bar, when I returned, had been similarly invaded. From the summer residence at Castelgondolfo to the Basilica of St. Peter, the mortal remains of Pope Paul VI, Supreme Pontiff of the Holy Roman Catholic Church were being transferred, and the color TV set above the bar was the cynosure of a hundred eyes. Talk was distracted and brief, uncharacteristically spare and simple as the plain papal coffin, now being borne into the entrance of Michelangelo's colonnade under the cameras of RTE.

Irish television had dispatched batallions of reporters to Rome for the live coverage, and one of them now spoke in a hushed and reverent voice in the manner of a baseball sportscaster during a slow game. "Famous for his extreme sensitivity and compassion, the Holy Father was deeply pained by the controversy which rocked the Church during his papacy. He wanted so very much for the people of the Church, for the people of the world. Peace was his greatest concern, and he agonized over the violence in Ireland, the country for which he had a special love, as he himself mentioned at the canonization of Blessed Oliver Plunkett. The members of the Swiss Guard are now . . . "

"Who's yer man in the middle there?" I looked away from the TV set at the man who had nudged me. The hash salesman hadn't even said hello. It was as if I'd never left.

"Who?"

"Yer man there. Behind the yoke."

I think he was talking about the most noticeable member of the procession, who, the RTE reporter had said, was Villot, the Vatican Secretary of State, because now, as the camera closed in on Villot, the hash salesman jerked his head towards the TV set, as if he were identifying a potential troublemaker in the pub. "That one."

"The guy on TV says he's Villot. The Secretary of State."

The salesman grunted. "Bollox." He sounded huffy.

"Pardon?"

"Behavin' like he's Pope already." It seemed to annoy the hash peddler that Villot, unelected by the conclave of cardinals, without the approval of the people of God, and untouched by the action of the Holy Spirit, should have the biggest hat.

"Just because he's wearing a mitre?"

"Not at all. It's all the attention they're payin' him. There, look." He jerked his head towards the set again, more annoyed than before. An acolyte was waving a thurible at Villot, who solemnly accepted the incense as if it were his due. The salesman was enraged. "Bollox," he said again.

I tried to reason with him. "After all," I said, "at this moment, at least until another pope is elected, he *is* for all practical purposes the pope. The TV guy just said that he was running the Church for the time being."

"Bollox." The salesman stared moodily into his Guinness, and I decided to change the subject.

"Where's Joe?"

"He'd a skinfull last night, and I doubt if he could stand the competition besides." A good point. One of Joe's stories would have been as inappropriate here, now, as it would have been during Mass. Even so, the profound absorption with which the Granby's patrons watched the television was surprising. Perhaps they were genuinely interested. Perhaps they felt it was their duty to interrupt the usual chatter to pay their last respects. Perhaps it was simply the presence of death. The salesman's involvement was the strongest of all, though. He did not, he admitted, consider himself a "good Catholic". Wondering what he meant by "good," I asked him if he meant that he didn't go to Mass every Sunday. It was as if I'd asked if he were a pederast; he was shocked. Of course he went to Mass every Sunday. That wasn't it at all. Well, what was it?

His mother was a good Catholic. All right, but what made her a good Catholic? He wasn't sure. She believed, though. Believed in what? In God. Didn't he? He did not. Wait a minute. He didn't believe in God, but he never missed Mass on Sunday? Never. I didn't understand. None of us Yanks did, he explained.

I still don't. Willing to defy the culture of the tribe at least enough to buy, sell, and smoke hash, willing to admit his defiance to Joe, to me, to the patrons young and old of the Granby Bar, willing to do in public a thing which his holy mother probably believed would damn him to hell forever, the hash salesman would never miss Sunday Mass, the worship of a God he did not think was there. And for all that, unwilling to give up the title "Catholic," he insisted that he was not a good one.

The subject had become uncomfortable, and the salesman changed it, ignoring, for the present, that uppity Villot.

"It's a fine, simple box they've put yer man

in anyway." If Florentine goldsmiths had crafted a coffin to dismay a Pharaoh, I'm sure the comment would have been equally enthusiastic. "Isn't that a grand sendoff they're givin' him, though?" Or something like that.

I agreed that the coffin was nice.

"Will they let him get all green, I wonder?" What on earth was this guy talking about? All green?

"All green?"

"Like Pope John. Ye remember?"

I remembered. Pope John had, apparently, not been embalmed. I began to wonder myself. On the television, the RTE reporter hadn't said anything about what they were going to do with the papal corpse. I told the salesman that I didn't know, and asked what he thought they should do.

"Let him get green, I'd say. When ye're dead, ye're feckin' dead, Pope er no. That John was a gas man, wasn't he? And green as the grass at the end."

"Did you like John better than Paul?"

"Gas man, he was. John was a fuggin' *Pope.*" Amazing. I was talking to an atheistic hash peddler who considered himself not a good Catholic, preferred, or seemed to, John the 23rd to Paul the Sixth, worried about Villot's imagined pomposity, and hoped that the dead pontiff would not be embalmed. All the hash dealers I knew at Notre Dame spent all their time reading Zap Comix and discussing narcotics laws. What would they think of this one?

What would anyone think? As the body of Paul, Servant of the Servants, was carried into the visible headquarters of our church, the salesman and I talked about local nuances. Few Catholics our age in my country, I told him, could even muster bitterness against the Church; I was confident that no hash salesman at Notre Dame was watching this proceeding, the widespread apathy of the age being what it was.

"It isn't like that here," he said. "The Church won't go away." The Guinness pints in front of us looked like twin priests. Black, with white collars.

State O'Chassis

*A*NY AMERICAN accepts it! The proper way to read *Time* is to begin at the back. Starting with the stern woman who looks like she'll crush your larynx with a hip kick if you question her Winston-smoking, you work your way forward to the portrait of Dolly Parton or Anwar Sadat. None of us questions these things. They will be explained someday, but we're not ready yet.

My application of this Yankee methodology to a reading of *In Dublin* might have been a mistake, but it yielded a significantly bizarre glimpse of contemporary Ireland's cultural and intellectual habits.

In Dublin (the "What's On Magazine") is published every other Thursday and is widely read by bored young students, middle class single folk, Bohemian-types, and American tourists alike. A mildly nihilistic, very drunk and disillusioned Marxist assured me that it was indispensible. So did a Benedictine nun. It seemed a good place to begin, and I did, with page 46.

Jansenist Ireland now can boast, if the classified ads are accurate, not only two massage parlors, but a gay women's disco, an oracle named Madame Joy (proficient in Crystal, Tarot and I Ching), and a Trinity College address at which contraceptives are available.

Michael Garvey

Page 45 reveals that there are dozens of young Dubliners with a broad range of sexual preferences, from the attractive girl who "with boyfriend's approval" wants to meet a "bisexual female between 18-30 to teach her the art of living", to the "sincere male student" who wants to form "a intellectual relationship with anyone. Perhaps a rare bird."

What is the reading taste of this exotic crowd? The book review section on page 43 contains a three-paragraph dismissal of Robbe-Grillet's *Topology of a Phantom City* ("This," says the critic, "is his seventh novel. I think it's a novel") and a six-paragraph treatment which makes me begin to doubt the accuracy of my investigations. The book reviewed concerns an event which took place near Dublin's Custom House around 3:00 a.m. on Friday, June 17, 1681. In case you've forgotten, that was the day when a large wooden booth was accidentally ignited, and its occupant, a bull elephant, perished in the flames. A Bachelor of Medicine at Trinity College became fascinated with the animal's corpse, and in 1682 published a book with the intriguing title: *An Anatomical Account of the Elephant Accidentally Burnt in Dublin on Fryday, June 17, in the Year 1681, Sent in a Letter to Sir Will Petty, Fellow of the Royal Society.* While the reviewer does not include the publisher or the price of the book, he mentions that it can be found in the National Library of Ireland. It is catalogued, should you be interested, under Mullen, and its call number is I.59941m.3.

All is far from well with urban Ireland, if the advertisements which separate the theatre reviews from the book section indicate the sufferings of Dublin literary society. Prominent among and typical of these is the promise of Mr. Terance Noble, M.B.S.H. Mr. Noble, a "consultant psychotherapist" and past President of the Irish Hypnology Society, will train you in self-hypnosis to rid yourself of enuresis and St. Vitus' Dance. But you are asked not to call on him without having made an appointment. I understand his request. What would you do if there were a sincere male student in love with a bedwetting parrot dancing with an anatomical account of an elephant corpse in your waiting room?

Offering constructive criticism for what he believes to be an inadequate production of Yeats' one-act play, *Purgatory*, the drama critic points out that "the use of coconut shells to create the ghostly hoofbeats and the use of a less busty female spectre at the window might have been a step in the right direction."

And then there is the meat of the issue.

Michael Garvey

Michael O'Leary, T.D. has written the most profound obituary for Elvis Presley to date. Quoting Eldridge Cleaver, James Joyce, and an unnamed French newspaper, O'Leary describes Elvis as largely responsible for the emancipation of Ireland from that "gerontocracy of Government and Church" which for years enabled traditional powers to enfetter creative expression.

Whether or not *In Dublin* exemplifies the free Irish expression which Elvis left in his wake, whether or not it accurately reflects current Irish literary interests, whatever the direction and object of its attention, it certainly makes of Ireland a deeper complexity. Or perplexity.

*a*LONG with a few more useful things I
inherited from my ancestors an instinctive mistrust of priests. Although anticlericalism and
orthodoxy are far from incompatible (an attractive argument might be made to demon-
strate their interdependence) their simulta-
neity in one human experience makes for all
sorts of burdensome distractions. Although
disliking priests is a natural and effortless
exercise for most layfolk, it is an exercise
which the practice of our faith demands we
forgo, not because they are virtuous, but because God loves even them.

So I've struggled long and hard against my
anticlericalism, meeting with occasional and
modest success. I'm afraid I can't avoid saying
it: some of my best friends are priests.

None of my best friends, at this writing, is a
bishop. Contempt for bishops, that most understandable and rationally compelling of all
vices, is an obstacle which must be confronted
eventually by any observer of the breed.
"Pigs," said one clerical friend of mine after a
particularly disheartening episcopal appointment, "beget pigs."

Nevertheless, Bishop-watching (which is
synonymous, after all, with Bishop-disliking)

Michael Garvey

consumes far too much time and effort in the discussions, writings, and thought of contemporary Catholicism, but then we have far too many bishops as well. America is a bishop-watcher's paradise, and since the late sixties our country has enjoyed a number of spectacular sightings. Bishop-watchers from all over the Western World flocked here for a glimpse of the ultimate bishop, and it's unnecessary to list their many striking discoveries, now commonplaces in the world of episcopology.

However, St. Patrick's College, Maynooth, is to bishop-watching what the city of Pamplona is to bullfighting. When I told one friend of mine, a professional episcopologist, that I would travel to Ireland, he urged me to visit Maynooth if for no other reason than to urinate on its walls. There, he said, one could site the ultimate bishop. (The ultimate bishop, my friend explained, was not a fixed or permanently identifiable entity. Any bishop is potentially the ultimate bishop, and the shiftings of history, theology, society and politics can bring out the various aspects of his plumage.) I asked my friend why Maynooth was the place; he would only say that Maynooth's "conditions were most favorable."

Like so many of Ireland's problems, Maynooth is a British invention. Its history begins during the reign of George III when Parliament, indulging a brief spasm of benevolence, passed a special piece of legislation, "an Act for the Better Education of Persons Professing the Popish, or Roman Catholic religion." This product of Brittania's maternal concern for her Irish Catholic children gave birth to St. Patrick's College, Maynooth.

It was about time. In those days, even after the Relief Act of 1793, to be an Irish Catholic was "a complex fate". You were allowed to vote for any antiCatholic parliamentary candidate of your choosing, but the substance of the required oath precluded your taking a parliamentary seat. You were allowed to attend Trinity College in Dublin (if you were unusual enough to be able to afford the tuition), but scholarships and faculty seats were denied you. And provided that the practice of your religion was confined within church walls, you were allowed to go to Mass.

Parliament's unexpected burst of goodwill caught Irish Catholics by surprise, and Maynooth was soon overrun by clerics, becoming, for all practical purposes, a seminary. In 1908, St. Patrick's College was recognized by the newly accomplished Irish Universities Act as a college of the National University of Ireland, and even today is subsidized by a million pounds of government money each year. Until 1966 Maynooth remained a seminary; then, the forces unleashed by the Second Vatican Council forced its gates open. Today lay students outnumber seminarians three to one, there are more women there than men, half the faculty have not received Holy Orders, and, if a recent poll is to be believed, twenty percent of its students say they are exCatholics.

The place is still run as a seminary. Seventeen Irish bishops make all decisions concerning college policy; they hire and fire teachers, they set academic requirements, they matriculate, graduate and expel whom they choose. Conditions for Bishop-watching at Maynooth are ideal.

While I was in Ireland, Irish newspapers were full of something called "the Maynooth case," a three-and-a-half year old controversy at least as complicated and furious as the Ulster situation and involving a few of the same ingredients. Among the contributors to the Maynooth case were seventeen bishops, the Irish judiciary, an academics' labor union, a papal encyclical, a major newspaper, the Second Vatican Council, and the first academics' strike in Irish history.

It began in 1975, on a quiet, dull, wet October morning in the rooms of one Father Patrick McGrath, a logic professor employed by St. Patrick's College, Maynooth. Imagine

State O'Chassis

Father McGrath having brushed his teeth and completed his shave, frowning into a mirror and pulling the last Kleenex-twist from a razor nick. He's in a lousy mood, perhaps having grazed an ingrown toenail while pulling on a sock, perhaps anticipating a boring, chilly journey to some poorly-lit and drafty lecture hall overcrowded with dull-witted, insolent, inattentive and twenty-per-cent fallen away students who are reluctantly completing logic requirements. He holds in his hand his wardrobe's single remaining clean collar, the others being overstarched, at the moment, by quiet Ursuline laundresses, or perhaps having been stolen by some practical joker who has burglarized his apartment. The collar may be a half-size too small for him, or there may be the first flush of a rash appearing around the young priest's neck. A well-meaning American relative has overlooked or ignored Maynooth's dress code, perhaps, and sent McGrath an attractive necktie. Recently he may have seen a Marlon Brando film in which an open collar looked particularly macho, or he's discovered that his more insolent students employ his collar as the root of some derisive nickname ("penguin-head" has appeared carved on a desktop, or "ringnecked dolt" has been overheard in the cafeteria). For whatever reason,

Michael Garvey

a foultempered member of the philosophy department snorts, flings the unused collar across his bedroom, and storms out of his rooms muttering syllogisms to himself. An ecclesiastical earthquake results from this small tantrum.

Sensitive episcopal trustees detected the first tremors, and the late Cardinal Conway immediately sent a letter to the epicenter. "Members of the staff," Conway thundered, must "resume the wearing of the clerical collar forthwith". Replying that he intended to seek laicization, McGrath remained obstinately naked. The bishops were furious, and across the world, Bishop-watchers quit their uninteresting local projects and turned their eyes toward Maynooth.

Soon, perhaps fearing an epidemic of secularism, the bishops went on the offensive. By Spring, 1977, McGrath had been asked for his resignation, not only because of his unconscionably nonclerical dressing habits, but also because of public expressions "prejudicial to the ecclesiastical authority", most notably an *Irish Times* article which had significantly deviated from the teachings of *Humanae Vitae*. Malachy O'Rourke, a teacher of modern languages at the college, had around the same time announced his intentions to leave the priesthood. The bishops suggested that he leave Maynooth while he was at it. Neither one of these rebels would resign, and on May 10th of that year, both of them were fired, apparently in response to the first academic strike in Irish history. The Irish Federation of University Teachers, which had arranged the strike, took the case to court.

The fact that while I was in Ireland, McGrath and O'Rourke were unemployed leads me to suspect that the bishops won. But a number of events intriguing to episcopologists had taken place. Among other things, the judgment of the High Court had been painfully prolonged while harried Latin scholars performed the tedious duty of translating Maynooth's antique statutes into sensible English. Vast amounts of court time had been consumed by a debate about the meaning of the phrase "clerical garb". College lawyers had at one moment requested additional time to examine a few fine points of canon law, and the impatient judge, Justice Hamilton, had irreverently suggested that the Holy Spirit be called upon for clarification. Although in the case of McGrath, the court had scolded the college for its failure to cite the real reason for his dismissal, it asserted nonetheless that "the continued employment of a priest who has become laicized is contrary to the interests of the college as a seminary."

The stunned Irish Federation of University Teachers seemed to regard the High Court ruling contrary to the interests of the college as a college, and accordingly called on the government to enact legislation distinguishing between Maynooth seminary and Maynooth college. Meanwhile, back at the college, two faculty members in line for promotion failed to get them. Unwisely, they had supported the IFUT strike, and vice presidencies were bestowed upon two happy priests who had supported the bishops. Evidently, the Church may boast seventeen bishops courageous enough to take a stand, even so vital a stand as insistence on proper priestly attire.

Whether or not the courage of these Irish bishops is reassuring, it is certainly beneficial to America. Increasingly, prominent faculty members from St. Patrick's College are appearing in American universities. Four of these immigrants are theologians, and one of them, Enda McDonagh, is considered by many to be Ireland's most brilliant. Father McDonagh's departure from Maynooth caused one intelligent commentator, Donal Ellis, to conclude that "Irish theology is now in the position of a chronically anemic individual who has just suffered a severe hemorrhage."

This is not the first time Irish theology has been convulsed by a trivial thing. Disagreements on the date of the Paschal celebrations and the appropriate size and shape of the priestly tonsure threatened schism centuries ago. McGrath's bad mood one wet October morning might someday dwarf the importance of the Second Vatican Council. The past in Ireland indeed happens over and over again.

Michael Garvey

IN THAT valuable and fascinating essay, "Why I Am a Catholic," G. K. Chesterton argues the futility of abandoning the Church. The worst aspects of corrupt Catholicism, he says, were made even worse in the new religion of those who rejected Catholicism. An expansive historical view brought him to this conclusion about the Reformation, and the conclusion is easily accepted by lazy-minded orthodox folk, a group in which I must include myself. But descending from Chesterton's exhilarating historical altitudes, to the small, individual human life, with all its particularity and goofiness, you can still see the tragedy of the leaving.

God has many surprises for us, and his ways are confounding and inscrutable; the earlobes of John XXIII, the invention of the codpiece, Jerry Lewis, and hamsters are just a few examples. In retrospect, the revelation of that tragedy through a concurrence of Raymond Chandler's writings, an alleged survivor of a Rhodesian atrocity, and the story of a broken-hearted ex-seminarian, does not seem unusual. But let me explain.

I was fantasizing in Sinnot's, a comfortable Georgian Dublin pub, that I was a disillusioned C.I.A. agent recovering from a cathartic, very dangerous mission, and waiting for Joni Mitchell to arrive for the resumption of our shattered love affair. She never showed up, but, as if to underline the unreasonableness of the fantasy, a hardfaced, angry-looking longhair entered the pub and took the stool next to mine.

He looked like he might have been a biker, a Trinity student, an actor, or an advertising executive; whatever else he was, until he began to explain the origin of the swastika tatooed on his right thumb, the fact that he was completely insane had not been apparent. Expressions of fierce emotion passed across his face like the shadows of clouds as he muttered that the symbol was "eighty times older than Christ." When did he get the tattoo? After Rhodesia, he said, adding that he didn't want to talk about it anymore.

And so, he began to talk about it. It was a religious symbol, the swastika was, that went back to the time of Caesar, Julius Caesar, and it didn't belong to the Nazis at all, although they took it for their own because that had been ordained long ago, thousands of millions of years ago, and he knew that he had to take it for his own after he was a missionary in Rhodesia. Yes, he had been a missionary in Rhodesia and a great believer at the time, too, until he saw those bloody bastards murder four nuns, each one getting a bullet right through the how's your father and himself pretending to be dead and God not anywhere to be found or at least not saying where He was and that day, that bloody moment, he stopped believing in God and that day, that bloody moment, he got this (pointing to the tattoo) and this (brushing back the hair on the side of his head to display a small earring) and God help the man who tried to take either of them away from him.

I wouldn't have dreamt of trying to take them away from him but as the barman, alert for any potential disturbance, watched with mild but undisguised hostility, the missionary glared at me, as if I were about to rip the ring from his earlobe and the dyed flesh from his right thumb. Joni Mitchell, obviously, would not show up to bail me out. To change the subject would be to admit the suspicion that the madman was talking to his hat; to pursue the subject would be, at best, disastrous; to allow the uneasy silence to continue would not only be awkward, but unkind. I was examining all these possibilities and becoming miserably aware that by hesitating for so long, I'd chosen the awkward and unkind silence, when he asked me if I'd have another drink. Again, it was difficult to respond.

But not too difficult. Thank you very much, I said, but this one must be my last. I have to be moving along.

"Please." The missionary had seized my arm, and seemed almost to be begging. Glancing at the barman, and in a lowered voice, he said, "Your man knows I'm daft, Friend, and you'll be putting the bad news on me if he thinks I've driven you off." I sat down again, pretending that I certainly didn't feel that the lunatic had driven me off, and having no idea what to say as this strangely lucid moment passed for him; he resumed his monologue. In a sharp voice he asked me why I ate pub grub. Feeling guilty, I stared at the crumbs of the cheese sandwich on the plate in front of me and tried to formulate a defense. Before I could answer, he began to recite a list of things I should and should not do. I should not eat pub grub, nor depend on bed and breakfast places; I should, as he did, take my meals for little or nothing from the Sisters of Our Lady of Good Counsel; I should bathe at Trinity Colege, ingratiating myself first with the students there by hanging around the Buttery; I should sleep on warm days in the Garden of Remembrance, and on cold nights in parked cars; I should in any case leave Dublin as soon as possible.

Michael Garvey

I asked why, and he became enraged again.
"Did I not just tell you where I got this (the
tattoo) and this (the earring)? Jesus, you ask an
army of questions, you! Do you see these
hands?" He lunged forward to show them to
me, ignoring, or failing to see my flinch. I did
see them. "Beautiful things, are they not?"
They certainly were. "Do you know why
they're beautiful?" I did not. "Because they've
never worked." Remarkable. "Do you know
why they've never worked?" I'd been about to
ask that. "Because I don't ask so many bloody
questions is why."

Another tense silence fell upon us as the
barman's annoyance visibly deepened and the
madman's emotions visibly multiplied. It would
have been inappropriate to put the question to
either of them, so I put it silently to myself.
Why did I encounter lunatics wherever I went,
and why so many in Ireland?

Several reasons, all too embarrassing to list,
were easily and immediately found for the first
part of my question. For the second part, there
were only a few theories:

1. The Jansenist structures of religion and
society which (until very recently, accord-
ing to some people, and even today, accord-
ing to others) unreasonably repress the

sexual instinct. Few young men, for example, continue to receive the Blessed Sacraments after they've reached the age of puberty. Appearances at the Communion rail of anyone but old ladies and old men are rare. To grow into adulthood certain that because you have thought, seen, heard, felt, or enjoyed just about anything, you were cut off from the faith outside which, as most of your teachers would tell you, there could be nothing but despair and damnation would, unless you were totally insensitive, drive you insane.

2. Brain damage from alcohol, due to the centrality of drink (because of number 1) in Irish culture.

3. A more humane approach to madness in Ireland. Most harmless loonies in Ireland, it seems, are permitted to remain on the streets and in the community, as opposed to our American system of hiding them in hospitals or asylums "for their own good."

4. The physical smallness of the island and its buildings which compresses the family and makes human relationships correspondingly intense and inescapable.

5. The fact that arrogant Americans (like yours truly) and pedantic Irish folk (like the author of every other letter to the Irish Times) are forever imagining and analyzing that useful thing called "the Irish character." When taken seriously by the weary or troubled mind, this fiction can lead to schizophrenia.

Still afraid to ask him about it (or about anything else), I wondered if this madman was a special case. Had he been born crazy, or had he really undergone some terrible experience in Rhodesia which had caused him to lose his reason along with his faith? Or had he simply rejected his faith and built the story around the ensuing pain, the way King Lear dressed himself up? Did his loss of faith cause his madness, or was it madness that made him lose his faith? He couldn't have been any worse off if he'd remained a Rhodesian missionary and a believer. He did not seem to be a happy man. And he had finished his drink, placing me, through the custom of rounds, in a doubly uncomfortable position. I owed him a drink, but doubted that the barman would serve it; if he had another, he would, without a doubt, go even crazier. Nothing pleasant would come of this.

Fortunately, the madman had another fit of

lucidity. "I'm shoving off, Friend," he whispered. "But I should confess that I'm a bit short. Could you ever part with the price of your pint? Only don't let your man see you give it to me, or I'll be barred from here."

I was relieved as I gave him the money and as we exchanged lies about seeing each other again. As he stood up, the sane spell broke suddenly, and he left the bar hissing "priest!" at a startled patron near the end of the counter.

"That," said the barman as he removed the missionary's emptied pint glass, "was a rare flower."

Priest moved up the counter from his place near the door, occupying the madman's stool and agreeing in an abnormally loud voice with the barman, "A rare flower, indeed. Did you hear what he called me?" Apparently the barman hadn't heard Priest, who then turned to me.

"Did you hear what that lunatic called me?"

"Priest, wasn't it?"

"Priest it was. Do you mind if I join you?"

I restrained myself from asking "Are you nuts?", and we started to talk.

Along with his other equipment, the half-finished pint of ale, the ashtray and Majors, and his umbrella, Priest brought an opened paperback edition of Raymond Chandler's *Farewell, My Lovely*; this must have been the source of the jarring hard-boiled-detective expressions with which his conversation was sprinkled, and which, uttered in the Georgian atmosphere of the place, gave a tense, surrealistic edge to the whole situation.

In his late twenties, curlyhaired, bespectacled and pudgy, Priest, or Sean McCafferty, as he later introduced himself, had been particularly upset by the missionary's epithet because he had left the seminary a few years ago. He divulged this information with exaggerated nonchalance, like an ex-convict applying for a job. As he watched for my reaction out of the corner of his eye, it was impossible to determine which thing he was bothered by, having gone to the seminary in the first place, or having left. Whatever he may have read in my reaction, it later seemed that he was bothered by both.

"Do you know why I left?"

"Of course not. Why?"

"A dame." That had to be from Raymond Chandler. What would he say if I replied, "You mean a bird?"

"You mean a bird?" When he didn't laugh, when he didn't even blink, I began to feel foolish. But I don't think he took any notice of my clumsy handling of a foreign idiom; he was bleary-eyed with the memory of something, and as he began to speak, it seemed almost as if he were in a trance.

"The mother wasn't what you'd call delirious with happiness at my decision, but the old fella was a brick altogether." He was the product, he said, of a "fiercely Catholic" family, although he himself was "not a very good Catholic."

Was anyone in Ireland a good Catholic? Every layman seemed to prefix every discussion about anything related to the Church, morals, patriotism, family, or personal belief with that admission. It could be the inordinately high standards set by the droves of Irish saints; they would be good Catholics. It could be the continuum of guilt which seemed to ensphere the island; only the Pope, and two or three nuns could make the claim to be good Catholics. Or maybe the admission was a formality, heartfelt as "sincerely" at the end of a business letter, a phrase without which it would be impolite to approach this important subject. Remembering the disgust with which the hash salesman had responded when I asked if it meant he didn't go to Mass every Sunday, I decided not to further bruise Sean's feelings. He had, after all, already been a priest that evening. Was he not a good Catholic because he had fallen in love with a dame? I didn't have to ask; Sean had been drinking lots of ale, and seemed inclined to chat.

"I'll always love the Church; don't get me wrong. It's only that the Church doesn't always love me or my kind."

Now what could he mean by that? The Church didn't love spoiled priests? The Church didn't love Chandler fans? The Church didn't love dame lovers? The Church didn't love spectacle-wearers, or ale drinkers? I asked him.

"Irish speakers."

I began to feel uneasy, as I had with the Rhodesian missionary, to imagine that he and Sean were roommates at the same asylum; that was why the missionary had hissed "Priest" at him; that was it, they'd both murdered an orderly and had, in the sharing of their guilt, begun to hate each other. Sean had followed the Rhodesian here to kill him, and the Rhodesian had defended himself by hissing the one word that could, like an amulet, protect him. Irish speakers, indeed. Like St. Patrick? Like three-quarters of the parish priests in Cork, Kerry, Clare and Donegal? Like Archbishop O'Fiach? There were rumors that Pope Paul, before his death, had decided to make O'Fiach a cardinal. If the Church didn't love a cardinal . . .

"Did you say Irish speakers?"

"You heard me, pal." (Chandler again.)

"How can you say that, Sean?" What about St. Patrick? What about Dr. O'Fiach? The Church doesn't love them?"

"*Irish* speakers, I mean. *Real* Irish speakers, I mean."

"You mean that those guys are not real Irish speakers?"

As an enormously restrained schoolteacher would explain to a petulant pupil a very simple problem, Sean defined a "real Irish speaker." A real Irish speaker, he said, was first of all fluent in Irish. Did I understand so far? I did. Good. And secondly, he was one who would refuse, under any circumstances whatsoever, to speak a different language.

"Like English, Sean?"

"Exactly." He sounded almost triumphant.

"But, Sean, unless I've gone mad, you're speaking English now!"

Sighing, and letting his shoulders drop as if he'd just given up supporting a gigantic weight, he stared gloomily into the bar mirror. "I know. Isn't that depressing?"

Well, it certainly was confusing. That the Church did not love real Irish speakers, even as Sean defined them, I seriously doubted, but that he could so passionately defend his own membership in that group, and in English, and in English peppered with Chandlerisms . . . that was a puzzle. And that he not only discerned, but obviously brooded over, the inconsistency of the whole thing . . . that made him seem less crazy than I'd suspected, and I felt an immediate kinship with him.

In silence, he continued to stare into the back-bar mirror, waiting, I guess, for his sadnes to pass. Then, jolted by a memory, he brightened quickly and said: "The old fella was a brick, as I think I told you."

"When you announced your decision to marry?"

"When I announced my decision to leave."

"The seminary?"

"The Church."

"Oh." Again, like the hash salesman. The old fella, Sean hastened to add, was not a very good Catholic either. His mother, as the hash salesman's mother, was a good Catholic. As he told stories about his fiercely Catholic family, the figure of Sean's mother emerged as pietistic, two-dimensional, domineering, and predictably narrowminded. It seemed that he despised her as he told of her disapproval of the shape his life had taken. How she thought of the girl he married as a whore, a sort of priest-stealer; how she considered proof of the girl's low morals the fact that Sean had no children; how she hadn't spoken to him until a year ago, and then only to berate him for his amoral life. What did his wife think of all this?

"Haven't a clue," Sean said. "We've been divorced a year now." And again the exaggerated casual tone, and again the furtive look. Did he expect me, I wonder, to fling my pint glass at him, scream, "I won't drink with a spoiled priest and adulterer!" and storm out?

"Do you know why we're divorced?" This was getting embarrassing.

"No."

"She thinks I still want to be a bloody priest." Poor Sean. Poor Ireland. Poor everything.

What could I say? I stared with him into the bar mirror, wondering if he wanted me to say something about that, wondering if he wanted to say something more, waiting for the gloom to lift.

And it did, again, with the memory of the old fella, who had been such a brick. One illustration of this quality was Sean's story of how he and his father had gone for a drink to a pub in their small Co. Clare village. The publican had brought them one drink, saying that he'd serve the old fella, but not the spoiled priest. Restraining the old fella from murdering the publican, Sean coaxed him finally out of the bar, and the old fella has never gone back there since.

Another illustration: Sean was sitting at home one day, alone in the parlor with his father. His father looked up from the newspaper and asked Sean, out of the blue, if he'd ever had the clap. Sean said he had, once. His father had grunted and continued to read the paper, looking up moments later to ask, "Did you get it taken care of?" Sean said he did, which seemed to satisfy the old fella, who never brought it up again.

Did these things make his father "not a very good Catholic," or did they make his father loving and loyal in a way that his mother was not? It was hard to tell what Sean thought as he told story after story about the old fella, his voice trembling and his eyes sometimes filling with tears. His father had died a year ago, he said.

Maybe that's what Sean liked about Chandler. There is always a sadness in Philip Marlowe's past, some large and unnamed suffering infecting the entire Los Angeles environment. With Chandler as your master, what better city than Dublin for sadness? Lousy weather, rivers of Guinness, and omnipresent guilt; dove-grey Georgian buildings to remind you of pretension and impotence; churches all over the place to remind you of lost innocence; and labyrinthine, mysterious streets to make your futile escape attempts interesting. If pain were an art form, Sean would be a genius, and it seemed this evening, as the gloom resettled, that he was engaged in the creation of a masterpiece.

It was flawed in a couple of places, though. True, he'd lost the Church, his vocation, his father, and his wife, but from the wreckage, he'd managed to preserve his job teaching Irish in a secondary school. Had it not been for a temporary shortage of competent Irish teachers at the time he left the seminary, even that would now be held by "some sap from the Christian Brothers." Chandler again. The contempt of the free-lance investigator for the flatfoot or the uniformed member of the L.A. force for which he'd once worked. It seemed that Sean now, adrift in the world outside the Church, was contemptuous of those regulars who confronted the same tragedies and ambivalences with the assurance of regular hours, societal sanction, and guaranteed pension. He ingurgitated the rest of his ale. "It's not all that bad, though," he said. Not knowing what else to do, I agreed, but the gloom persisted.

"I'm living in sin with another broad now."

Michael Garvey

I burst out laughing, dazzled by the discordance in the sentence; Aloysius of Gonzaga on a roller derby team, Mother Teresa wearing falsies, Cardinal Carberry in a leisure suit, Hans Kung wearing a toupee . . . delicacy and vulgarity in goofy imbalance. Noticing that Sean wasn't laughing, that the strange sentence wasn't meant to be funny, and that, far from lifting the sadness, the statement had somehow confirmed it, I felt, once again, like an idiot. But "living in sin"? This guy, who only moments ago had been satirizing his mother's piety? A Chandler character might, at least, have said "shacking up with another broad". Sean's mother, I'm sure, would have said "living in sin with some strumpet". But it seemed that the sentence reflected Sean's inability to decide between two cosmologies.

"Do you really think it's a sin?"

"There isn't any such thing." (Sean, dogmatic humanist.)

"Then why do you use the word?"

"We're not married." (Grammarian?)

"You could say 'we live with each other'."

"But we shouldn't be living together." (Secular moralist?)

"Do you think it's wrong?"

"I don't love her." (Lapsed Catholic.)

Closing time, and the gloom had reached suicidal depths. I had to go.

But Sean still wanted to talk. "It's early; let me show you where I live." Suddenly, he was cheerful again. The broad with whom he was living in sin, would she mind if we woke her up at this hour? He was gloomy again. "She's out of town at the moment. We won't have to worry on that score, anyway."

We had to take a taxi to get there. The fact that Sean had frequently referred to Sinnot's as his "local" surprised me; he lived miles away from the City Center. I began to wonder if the broad with whom he lived in sin were fictional, an invented flourish to embellish the tragedy he almost seemed to enjoy. But as he spoke about her, it became obvious that no fantasy, not even in Ireland, could generate as much guilt as had their relationship.

"When she comes back, I'm going to break it off," he said, "and that'll be hellish. She suspects it, I think, although we've never brought it up with each other; she loves me, you see. How can I tell her?"

Sean's apartment was a large unit of one of those sprawling fake-Tudor housing complexes like you see on the outskirts of American cities. Black vinyl, mobile-home furniture, flecked and ruffled plaster walls, indoor-out-door carpeting and a kitchenette-bar in the living room. Even a garbage disposal, about which he couldn't resist the boast, "very American and modern."

There was not, apparently, any aspect of his life uninfluenced by his fascination with pre-world-war-two private eyes; he found a bottle of bourbon (in Dublin!), waved it at me and said, "Hell with the tea. Wanna slug?"

But not even Chandler could keep his mind off the Church; as we sat in the living room, he would speak of no other thing. Except sex.

The whole problem, as he saw it, was that for "them," sex was a sort of ethical fulcrum, and they used it as the center for any moral problem. "Sex," he said as if in disbelief, "the most shadowy, vague area of human person-ality!" Poor Sean. Not for him, it wasn't. He could talk of little else.

Because of his free-thinking attitudes, he had a great rapport with his students, he said. One of them, a worried teenage girl, had come to him in his office one day. Unable to confide in her parents, her pastor, or any of the other teachers, she asked him a question which had been plaguing her for weeks. Would she be-come pregnant if she allowed her boyfriend to touch her breasts?

This was too much. "I simply don't believe that, Sean."

"I swear to God, it's the truth," he insisted, adding, "but listen to me. Swearing to God, and I don't even believe in him. But listen, that's not the important part of the story." He had told her, he said, as delicately but as honestly as he could, how babies were made. Somewhat relieved, she'd gone on to talk about how much she loved her boyfriend, and how much she believed he loved her. Should she let him go that far?

"Do you understand what I'm telling you?" Sean was almost weeping now. "The poor dumb thing had to come to somebody for *permission*, for Christ's sake. She wanted my *permission* to do something that wasn't my business, nor anyone else's except hers and her boyfriend's. She wanted me to say 'yes, you may do that' or 'no, you may not.' Because I was some form of authority. She couldn't decide on such a simple, personal thing as that by herself. That's what they *do* to you!"

"But isn't that what "they" do to you everywhere? In any culture, in any religion, in any family?"

He was absolutely positive: "Not like they do it here, in Ireland. Not at all like they do it here."

"So what did you say to her?"

"I told her to do anything she damn well pleased, provided that she didn't hurt herself, that she didn't hurt him, and that her own conscience was clear."

"Sounds pretty much like Church teaching to me." (It didn't sound much like Church teaching at all, though, except for the number of restrictions.)

Sean was nearly feverish with the argument. "It might. But remember *they've* got hold of your conscience. Your conscience would never be clear about anything sexual, even if you were married." Good point.

"So you're saying that you couldn't really help her out much?"

"I'm saying that nobody could help her out at all. She *believed* all that shit. They've made her a slave, I'm telling you. They do that to everyone, but they won't do it to me again. I've finished with that rot. Let's not talk about it. Slainte." He drank. Rabelaisian Sean, swigging bourbon, "living in sin with another broad," atheistic, "not a very good Catholic," liberating a guilt-ridden adolescent by telling her to enjoy life but keep her conscience clear, pretending to be Philip Marlowe at night and by day teaching teenagers the facts of life and the pagan joys of Celtic myth. Happy, free, life-affirming Sean. He had become very, very drunk.

As if we'd still been talking about her, the subject of his exwife came unexpectedly into his monolgoue. "Even when I'm with the other one, I'm still thinking about her all the time. Do you know why she left?"

"You said she thought you still wanted to be a priest."

"Well, there was that, of course," he said vaguely. "That was the main thing, to be sure. Yes, that was the thing, all right." He grew silent again, and seemed to have forgotten my presence, staring dully at the flecked wall. Time for me to go again, I thought.

But he snapped out of it suddenly. "On the end table, there, beside you. See that passport? Take a look at it, why don't you?" I did. "I came home early one afternoon and found that man in bed with her. I was so angry, shocked, really, and he was so frightened, that he left without it. She's with him now, I think." Again he fell into the silence for awhile, and then looked up with a twisted grin. "And what do you think of that?"

I suppose there were several things I could or should have said then. "Sean, you're a masochist, and you should see a psychiatrist;" or "Sean, I'm so sorry for you;" or "Sean, why the hell don't you go back to the Church. It wasn't the Church that made your wife unfaithful;" or "Well, Sean, ain't life a mystery?" But instead, perhaps unconsciously, or perhaps because I'd been in Ireland for too long, I found myself pronouncing the verdict of the Church, the family, and the Irish culture on Sean's pain, ambiguous as his advice to the teenage girl, ambiguous as the pain itself. A sharp, throaty inhalation.

When I left Sean's house, it was too late for cabs or buses. During the long walk back, there was, aside from the general misery of Sean's story, something bothering me. It didn't come to mind until I'd reached my bed and breakfast place. He had never explained why the Church does not love Irish speakers. In the rest of my travels in Ireland, I never heard anyone else make the accusation.

*t*HE PRIEST was in his seventies; slight, bald, and suspicious. His features brightened somewhat when he heard my accent, as if the fact that I was an American justified my hitchhiking; as if an Irishman of my age should be ashamed of himself for not working or studying, or being in a seminary. He was full of questions about the United States, and, like so many of the people I met, terrified of blacks.

"But they're quite hostile, I suppose, are they?"

"No more so than other people in the cities, Father."

"But are they not resentful for the old slavery days?"

And so forth.

There must be a reason for those fascinations and fears. The visit to Ireland of Mohammed Ali a few years ago quickly took on the proportions of a major national event; the sight of an intelligent, fierce, and outgoing black man convulsed some unnamable ethnic nerve. Thousands turned out in Dublin to watch "the neegers" (Blue Moon Otum fought Ali that night) slug at each other, and all in Ireland seemed much more comfortable with Mohammed Ali the fierce black buck than with

Michael Garvey

Mohammed Ali the Black Muslim and social critic. Even this old priest remembered watching the fight on television, and concluded, "Those neegers are right clowns, aren't they?" As with so many other problems, television must be largely responsible for the ignorance. The girl who had sold me a hamburger in Belfast was convinced that all American blacks were like the gang leaders and smack freaks portrayed on *Kojak*. A ten year old farmer's son in Kerry had asked me if the Indians were much of a problem for "people" in the United States. When I had asked him what he meant by a problem, he'd asked if they didn't attack white towns and cities.

But the old priest had other things to worry about this afternoon.

"You've been here before, have ye?"

"Yes, Father. Three times."

"Would ye not say it's changed a bit?"

"It seems to have changed a great deal."

"Oh, it has, I'd say. The young people becomin' much more materialistic, if ye want my opinion."

"But don't you think it's good that young people are staying in Ireland? That there are more jobs for them here, so that they won't be raising families in Boston, or Liverpool or someplace away from their home?"

He snorted. "Raisin' families did ye say? Most of 'em won't raise a family at all, with their Birth Control and all that they get from the North."

I didn't feel up to a debate about *Humanae Vitae* (and it would be years before I got another ride on this poorly traveled road) so I asked him if he didn't think that this present prosperity, even with all the moral complications, was better than the old cycle of poverty, emigration, and cultural drain.

"It is, I suppose. When you've a great amount of poverty, the people start to listen to the atheistic communists. But the young people have a right soft time of it these days all the same."

I asked him if he didn't consider capitalism to be just as atheistic, if not more atheistic than communism. He looked at me with a bitter smile and made a gesture with his left hand which seemed to indicate all Ireland.

"Only look around yerself, lad. Only look around."

He brooded for the rest of the ride.

Michael Garvey

"Although they be reported to be full
frought of lewde examples, idle tales and
genealogies . . . yet with choice and judgment I might have sucked thence some
better store of matter had I found an inter-
preter or understood their tongue."
— Edmund Campion
[on the subject of Irish fairy tales]

IN MY FAMILY, which is fond of argument,
the introduction of any rationally penetrable
problem assures intense and occasionally unpleasant controversy. Thus innocent questions—like could you fit a million dollars in
ones into the refrigerator? could you survive
more than fifteen minutes with a life-jacket in
February in the waters of the North Atlantic?
have there been any Chinese chess cham-
pions? carry volatile emotional freight.

When Dermot Hurst and his wife drove one
day this summer from their home in Dublin to
visit friends in Castledawson I'm sure they had
no idea that their trip would become historic.

They noticed, as they drove north, dozens of

dead crows lying beside the road, and they assumed that these were the result of heavy, rapid traffic. But at Newry, the midpoint of the journey and the frontier of the Six Counties, they noted a significant decrease in the number of crow corpses. Could it be that there were fewer dead crows in British-controlled Ireland? They decided to count them on the return trip, and the statistics confirmed their earlier observation. A mere 22 dead crows lay beside the road from Castledawson to Newry, while 98 were counted in the Republic, from Newry to Dublin. Dermot Hurst wrote a letter to the *Irish Times* a few days later, reporting the phenomenon and wondered if any *Times* readers could explain.

An E.M.B. Warren answered two days later that Hurst had "raised a problem in connection with crows over which I have brooded for years." Mr. Warren had noticed great numbers of dead crows on the road between Limerick and Dublin four years earlier and had at the time remarked to his wife that if this slaughter continued there would soon be no more crows in Ireland. He had, he admitted, seen dead crows on British roadsides before, but never anything on this scale. After asking several authorities in Britain and Ireland, he'd received no justification for the number, but had received a variety of speculations. The most plausible of these was that Irish farmers perhaps used some pesticide illegal in Britain, a pesticide which dulled the birds' reactions and made them slower in avoiding oncoming cars.

Four days later, Leslie N. Keegan thought not and explained why: The 98 crows slain in the Republic could be accounted for by "the much heavier transportation of grain by bulk carriers on that section of road," even a slight spillage of which will attract hundreds of crows "and result in a much higher mortality rate."

But Peter Fessler reported in the next issue of the *Times* that a lady friend had once told him the reason he felt so sleepy and peaceful in Ireland was a fermentation process in the omnipresent peatbogs. This evaporated a gas which pleasantly inebriated everyone on the island, and perhaps slowed down the odd, unfortunate crow as well.

R. H. Leahy then suggested that the argument was not moving in the proper direction. The difficulty was not with Irish crows at all, but with Irish drivers. And why, he wondered, did Irish seagulls seem to abandon car ferries within a mile or so of British ports? What were the British doing to the seagulls, or were they merely obeying territorial instinct?

Edna Gabb wanted more precision. There are only two species of crow (carrion and hooded) in Ireland, and neither of these are found (at least in great abundance) dead along Irish thoroughfares. No, in all likelihood, the birds discussed so far were jackdaws. While all three species belonged to the order Corvidae, we should nevertheless be more specific.

The Crow Count column in the letters page of the *Irish Times* was, by the time I left the country, very nearly an institution. Its contents were debated hotly in pubs from Dingle to Antrim, and I sometimes contributed to these debates my own theories and prejudices on the matter. But (not that this should influence the controversy) I can solemnly swear that never, in six weeks of travel in that country, did I see a dead crow. Or jackdaw. Or rook.

Michael Garvey

IT IS POSSIBLE, even in this turbulent age, to find inveterate materialists. To these happy folk, blissfully confident that there is not, nor ever can be, communion between the material and the immaterial, this useful exercise should always be recommended: Consider the Golden Arches.

A vision of the Gold Arches discloses specific and discernible quantity to those billions of hamburgers McDonald's has sold. Hamburgers, like mountains, whales and mousetraps occupy space and occur in time; billions of hamburgers can be weighed, measured, tasted and smelled. But to imagine, or to attempt to imagine what an arrangement of ten billion hamburgers would look like, to discover where they came from and to wonder where they've gone, it to bring the talents of mere human perception to the frontiers of the mystical. No rational being has ever entered a McDonald's free from awe at the enormity and strangeness of physical space. Up against the mystery of ten billion hamburgers, the material world becomes a frail and trembling thing, a material fart in a numinous typhoon.

This worries me. By the turn of the century, assuming that we avoid the logical outcome of the arms race, there will be, I'm sure, a

McDonald's in Peking and perhaps even on another planet. I am also convinced, although I could never prove it, that Mick Jagger, Jimmy Carter, Dan Berrigan, Saul Bellow, Alexander Solzhenitsyn and Pope John Paul II have all eaten, at some time in their lives, at least one item on McDonald's menu. I am as paranoid about McDonald's as Anita Bryant about homosexuality, or the Blue Army about communism, or a Dublin cop about speech. I see it as a capitalist plot.

The most disingenious psychologist of the twentieth century designed the McDonald's menu. For two months of my adult life I lived exclusively on McDonald's hamburgers and milkshakes, never really enjoying but always depending upon that limited fare. With every other American of the postwar generation, I am as familiar with the price list above the stainless steel counter as with the alphabet. Like every American of the postwar generation, I am unable to decide quickly between the Big Mac and the Quarter Pounder w/Cheese.

It was only after a long argument and the assurance that this was the only tourist-free restaurant in Dublin that I agreed to go with an Irish friend to the McDonald's in Grafton Street. (I share with all other tourists a distaste for tourists.) Although while we were there, I did not spot any other tourists, I accept that my friend's confidence in the unadulterated Irishness of the Dublin McDonald's patronage was unjustified. The Grafton Street McDonald's hadn't been there long enough for him to realize that nobody in the West, tourist or native, is able to stay away from McDonald's very long.

We had to circumnavigate a couple of Mormon evangelists to get into the place. Clean-cut and stay-pressed, eyes alert in a dancing search for optical contact, they looked like a pair of technological priests, there in front of McDonald's eager to introduce Old World natives to a sprawling, corporate way of doing things. They belonged there.

"I don't like this," my friend was muttering, as we avoided evangelization. "They're everywhere these days."

"Mormons?"

"All of them. Moonies, Jesus people, the whole lot."

He told me, as we waited in a long line for our chance to balk at the price list, that Dublin was lousy with street evangelists these days. If my brief time there was typical, he was right. In one afternoon on O'Connell Street, for example, I was approached by representatives of The Children of God, The Unification

Church, the Hare Krishna, and a Catholic sect calling themselves Mary's Followers of the Cross.

Whether or not any of these groups gain converts through their Dublin efforts, I can think of few better cities than Dublin for street-preaching. No matter how easy it may be for an urban Irishman to pass the dozens of beggars on Dublin streets, it is with great difficulty that he lets pass the opportunity for an argument, or a theological/political discussion. Passing two Children of God accosting a priest on the sidewalk, I heard a snatch of an exchange possible, it seems to me, only in Ireland. The priest, head thrown back and bespectacled screwed into an intense, scholastic expression, was saying, "heretical Gnosticism always gives way to such things." Small talk, as he waited for his bus. The poor Children of God were returning bleary-eyed smiles.

From the tinfoil, starshaped ashtrays on the tables to the last sesame seed on your Big Mac, the Grafton Street McDonald's is, of course, the duplicate of every other. My friend, who two years before had described a strawberry milkshake in a Canadian McDonald's as "poisonous," now ordered one to go with his Quarter Pounder, claiming that here they were different. McDonald's has learned from St. Columba, whose peculiar genius grafted Christian tradition onto local Celtic paganism, making an imported world-view seem compellingly indigenous; even the Mormons in front of the place proselytized in thick Dublin accents. Like the Normans, centuries before, deleterious technology and the American corporate onslaught had arrived, showing every indication that they would become "more Irish than the Irish themselves." Billboards on the "dual carriageway" entrance to Dublin now advertise Guinness with the slogan, "Black Is Beautiful;" there is a Kentucky Fried Chicken in Limerick; from Antrim to Kerry, every other sweet shop advertises "Genuine American Ice Cream;" transistor radios in pubs blare with loud commercials, screaming the capitalist litany. It was as if some cancerous Los Angeles spore had drifted far to the East, landing here in Ireland to find vulnerable soil, spreading weird American fungus through an unwary culture. Morose, I removed my Big Mac from its styrofoam container and started to eat.

Maybe all those whacked-out anthropologists who talked about "cultural materialism" were right. Maybe cultural forms, even in Ireland, were determined by the extent to which they catered to fleshly whim, so that the variety and redundance, the intricacy and goofiness of Dublin street life, the eccentric shops and pubs and cafes which delighted the Joyce-freaks and authenticity-lusting tourists were being sold for a mess of pottage, a Big Mac, large order of fries, and a coke. Grease, sugar, and mayonnaise are as addictive and deadly in Grafton Street as in Pocatello, after all.

But even here, in this sanctuary of everything that is wrong about the West, there was evidence that the Irish, so accustomed to invasion and conquest by the Norsemen, the Norman and the Briton, would never let this voluptuous threat get the upper hand. Perhaps still dazzled by the novelty of their McDonald's "hamburger restaurant," Dubliners seemed to linger over their cheeseburgers and filet-of-fish sandwiches. As they rattled ice cubes in the paper cups, chewed on the plastic straws, and folded up the tinfoil ashtrays, satiated diners chatting comfortably in the bathroom-tile atmosphere of the place seemed to be engaged in acts of passive resistance to the streamlined capitalist efficiency of mass hamburger production. The auditive battle between purring, clicking, Star-Trek digital cash registers and the syncopated cadences of Dublin speech was clearly being won by and for Old Ireland; so that at a nearby table, oblivious to the confusion and efficiency, a gaggle of old ladies could be overheard sharing the results of their investigation:

"Isn't it grand they've everything on them?"

"It is lovely."

"And these tops for the cups as well."

"Very sanitary, those."

"They've lovely crisp chips, haven't they?"

"They have."

"Here, look, mine's blood-red in the center. I'll take it back."

And so forth. Here, before atheistic capitalism had yet completed its conquest of Hibernia, the seeds of rebellion were already being sown. "We serve," said Ireland's patriots before World War One, "neither King nor Kaiser." Nor, it begins to seem, cheeseburger.

As we left the Grafton Street McDonald's, my friend and I had again to circumnavigate its Mormon sentries. This time we noticed a drunk man arguing with them.

O R. GILLIGAN made housecalls, drunk or sober. When I met him, hitchhiking through Sligo, he was making a housecall, drunk. Very drunk. But not so drunk that he was unable to recite the entire Gettysburg Address for me, his little car grazing the hedgeweeds beside the road at breathtaking intervals and his recitation occasionally punctuated (at those times death seemed closest) with prayers and blasphemies: " . . . now we are engaged in a— Jesus, Mary and Joseph, protect and guide us —great Civil War, testing whether—Christ on a bloody crutch—that nation or any nation..." And so on, from Tobercurry to a small farmhouse outside Ballynacarrow, where he bid me wait in the car while he attended "a poor old soul who suffers a great deal from what we call 'environmental depression.' " He left the engine running as he spoke briefly with a frightened-looking old woman on the doorstep of the house and disappeared within.

The interior of his car, I noticed during the fifteen minute wait, was littered with professional and recreational equipment, stacks of medical journals, unidentifiable cords of rubber tube, boxes of medicines and drugs, a device for measuring blood pressure, half a dozen potboiler novels, and a paperback, three-volume set of Sandburg's Biography of Abraham Lincoln.

The house door opened suddenly, and Dr. Gilligan emerged, still reassuring the frightened old woman, having apparently left scribbled and muttered instructions for the continued treatment of his depressed patient. Sighing, he threw back the car door and sat heavily on the driver's seat, causing the small car to jolt in his direction. "Well, that's done, praise God," said the Doctor. "Will we go for a drink?"

It was a polite opportunity to escape the car. The weavy spin north from Tobercurry had made me nervous; there had to be a pub within a mile or so of the farmhouse, so I consented. We lurched back onto the road, and the Doctor spoke for a few more miles of Lincoln's physiological predisposition towards melancholia. "As if the potential dissipation of the Union weren't enough to break the poor man's heart!"

Gilligan had a romantic fondness for things American. The Doctor had studied medicine in Boston and, in addition to the overwhelming courseload of a medical student, had taken a number of courses in American History. With the writings of Mark Twain, he was as familiar as a University of Missouri English professor, and he was full of questions about the Watergate scandal. Surprisingly, he seemed to dislike the Kennedy family. ("They betrayed their ancestry, the sycophants. All they wanted was power and prestige; that was the whole affair. They wanted to be like those—what do they call 'em—Boston Brahmins, if you want my opinion.")

As if to emphasize the seriousness of this accusation, Gilligan, with a ferocious wrench at the steering wheel, pulled his car off the road. The roar of cinders against rubber disrupted my pulse and made my joints feel watery. Chalk-like flakes of rearranged gravel dust swirled and settled about the car, and we could see through the haze an undecorated, almost neolithic-looking stone building beside the road. Seeming to suspect a mirage, the Doctor squinted through the dust a moment before grunting affirmatively and turning to me.

"Here, my dear man," he said in a didactic tone, "you may drink the finest pint of porter currently available in the Republic. Be sure of it, now." We both had to stoop (and I am not tall) to enter the interior darkness.

Two deep, descending steps brought us to a black, enclosed space about the size of a telephone booth; the Doctor pushed open a heavy wooden door whose movement activated a sharp, high-pitched bell.

Within, the place was only slightly better-lit, and gloomy after the bright weather outside. A single, naked lightbulb illuminated, or tried to, a small, drab room of murky brown walls and a grey cement floor. Dust heavily coated the greenish whiskey bottles on the back bar in weird contrast to a slick poster advertising Harp. The poster depicted a beautiful blonde woman, bikini-clad and healthy-looking, carrying a surfboard along a Mediterranean beach. We stared at her for a few uncomfortable, silent moments until an interior door beside the back bar opened slowly.

The publican, a large, quiet, brooding man was bald as a cueball, and without consulting the Doctor, he began to draw from the tap a brown and creamy pint. Staring at me solemnly as he did so, he scraped from the brim the first meniscus of foam and asked, "Same for you, Lad?" Except for the ticking of a grandfather clock, the place was silent, and the solemnity seemed to require respectful brevity.

"Same, please."

The Doctor drank half his pint slowly and with reverence, as if this were a sacrament.

The clock continued to tick, and the publican, apparently oblivious to our presence, sat quietly behind the bar, smoking a pipe. The silence of the place was full, rich, and comfortable, as if we were in a cathedral.

Gilligan set his half-empty pint glass on the bar with great gentleness, placed his elbows on either side of it, and began to massage his eyebrows. "That," he said quietly, "is a beautiful pint."

The publican inclined his head slightly toward the Doctor and inhaled sharply, making "the noise".

After another silent pint, the Doctor's mouth became suddenly filled with words. He spoke of the American West, quoting passages from the journals of Mountain Men, identifying bandits who robbed Wells Fargo, and describing the shootout at the O.K. Corral in such painstaking detail that the bar began to smell of dust, blood and sagebrush. He had always, he said, wanted to visit Taos, New Mexico, to see the square where Kit Carson ran up the Union flag and threatened to shoot anyone who attempted to strike it. "You've a grand country, Lad."

"So have you, Doctor Gilligan."

"Ireland? Oh, Ireland's a fine land, all right." There was something desultory about his approval, and the enthusiasm faded from his eyes.

"Why did you return from Boston?" The Doctor was silent, and the publican's expression was wooden. I wondered if I had asked too personal a question, and was too embarrassed to let it hang there in the silence. "I mean, you seem to love America, and you know more about it than most Americans do."

The Doctor grunted at his pint, and spoke. "Home, I suppose, and I'm able to do some good things here as well." That gloomy response, I knew, was the limit of what Dr. Gilligan would reveal. We were silent awhile.

"But you've heroes there," Gilligan was impassioned again, "real heroes. Lincoln, Kit Carson, Daniel Boone, Stonewall Jackson."

"But there are heroes here, too. Collins, Conolly, Wolfe Tone, DeValera, all those guys. They're all heroes, aren't they?"

The Doctor grew solemn. "In any bar in Sligo," he said, "you will find a half dozen conflicting opinions of the men you've just now mentioned."

"Not about Tone, ye will not." We both jumped slightly. The publican had spoken.

Hastily, the Doctor agreed. "True enough, Tom. Wolfe Tone was grand."

As if he hadn't heard, the publican spoke

again, "Wolfe Tone was a great Irishman."

The Doctor agreed once more. "He was, Tom. He was, surely." The publican was again silent. Satisfied that heresy had been successfully aborted, he relit his pipe.

The Doctor continued to speak, but now in a lower voice, as if fearful that the publican might overhear something unorthodox and throw us both out of his place. "Why do you think," the Doctor was almost whispering, "that in every country home, next to the picture of the Sacred Heart, you will find a picture of John and Jacqueline Kennedy? Why?" I gave up. Why? "Because, Lad, they're imported. They're Irish enough to be *claimed* by the people, but nobody knows enough about the Kennedys to call them anything but saints. The marriage of Jackie to that Onassis character: have you any *idea* of the impact on the country people? A friend of mine, a priest, made a remark when Jackie married again that 'at last the picture of the Sacred Heart will be restored to its proper place in every Irish home.' He's on to something, I'd say." If the Kennedys lived in Ireland, the Doctor thought, they could never have come to be so loved there.

"The qualifications of Irish heroism are unusual, Lad," Doctor Gilligan concluded.

"You must be one of two things: a foreigner or safely dead." He fell into silence. The grandfather clock chimed suddenly, jolting the publican from the chair in which he had fallen asleep as the Doctor spoke of death and greatness. He raised his eyebrows to offer us fresh pints, but we both refused, and like fine dust, gloom settled around the small room.

State O'Chassis

> "Not all psychologists know of fantasy as
> a modality of experience, and the, as it
> were, contrapuntal interweaving of dif-
> ferent experiential modes"
> The Politics of Experience
> R.D. Laing

*t*O QUALIFY a buoyant sentence with the phrase "as it were" might be to warn the reader that the statement's helium level has risen too sharply, and that a tenacious pursuit of its meaning could carry him up to a delirious orbit from which nothing can return.

So, for safety's sake, let's assume that R.D. Laing means this: fantasy, no less than sex, boredom, death-denial, and McDonald's hamburgers, permeates human experience; the psychologist who is unaware of this ignores an incontrovertible aspect of humanity.

If that is what Laing means, I think I agree with him. And, although in three days there, I never encountered a single psychologist, I would suggest that Laing consult the Belfast phone directory for colleagues who would be sympathetic to his views.

A Belfast psychologist who does not, in this sense, know of fantasy as a modality of experience simply isn't paying attention, or is perhaps absorbed in articles containing phrases like "as it were".

While I was there, Belfast seemed as fantasy-laden as Disneyland and different experiential modes were contrapuntally interweaving all over the place. Disgorged from the strict security checks at the Central Railway Station into the ugly urban frenzy of Albertbridge Road, I was instantly caught in the hallucinogenic web. Belfast was like something Dickens would describe in *Hard Times,* and its unrelenting greyness would naturally inspire a tourist or a native to deploy a sort of imaginative guilt. How, in such a drab city, could there be any sort of territorial imperative at work? Who would want a single street here? Among the thousands of conceptions of Ulster's war, the Belfast poet Seamus Heaney has contributed the notion of a standoff between two goddesses, Cathleen Ni Houlihan—pagan, wild, anarchist and, of course, Catholic—and the Queen of England—rational, orderly, imperial and Protestant.

Cathleen, at least in my fantasy, could not be at home on this battlefield. As I wandered toward the City Centre past the swollen Georgian architecture of the City Hall, it seemed that long ago the Industrial Revolution had become an institutional church, and that this feverish-looking building was its Vatican. I decided not to stay in Belfast long.

At the northern edge of the City Centre, I found a long line of people waiting for seats in the famous Black Taxis. It was late in the afternoon, and the business district was emptying rapidly. One man seemed to be in charge of the line, organizing irritable workers and shoppers by their destinations, shouting out the street names which are now famous . . . Crumlin Road, Upper Falls Road, Lower Falls Road, Antrim Road, etc. Each departing taxi seemed to contain a dozen noisy passengers who knew where they wanted to go. Feeling once again like an idiot Yank, I approached the man shyly, asking if he could recommend a Bed & Breakfast. He reciprocated with a look which assured me that I was, in fact, an idiot Yank, and in the annoyed tone a parent uses with a child who has done something irremediably disruptive, ordered me to stay put.

Moments later, to my deeper embarrassment, I was the sole passenger of an angrily driven Black Taxi, staring guiltily at the neck of the driver and pretending not to notice the outraged gazes of a hundred waiting citizens. I'll leave tomorrow, I thought.

"American, are ye?" No. Tanzanian. Can't you tell?

"Yes. Davenport, Iowa." In the silence that

followed, I became miserably aware that I'd committed the most common American neocolonialist sin, the assumption that everyone knows one's town; that because I'd spoken its name this inconvenienced Belfast native would respond: Davenport? Yeah, I know, the Mississippi River, O'Donnel Stadium, the Centennial Bridge. The assumption that Ulster was the fifty-first state.

"Well, Davenport, I wouldn't describe our tourist industry as booming at the moment." Nervously, in the wake of his sarcasm, I inhaled sharply, making "the noise." The attempt to find a Bed & Breakfast had become uncomfortable enough without the extra baggage of my Midwestern accent, and I'd decided to be discreetly taciturn.

We finally found a place, far up the Antrim Road. In the front hall, a matronly woman with a crisp British accent stood beneath a huge portrait of King William. "And how long will you be staying with us?" Was there disaproval in her tone? I couldn't tell.

"Only tonight," I said.

Several Irish friends had told me that I would be astonished by the normalcy of Ulster life, and, so far, despite the omnipresence of sullen, adolescent British soldiers, despite the three polite, firm, and thorough searches to which I, with my knapsack, had been subjected that afternoon, despite the frequent sight of whorled razor-wire, and despite the fierce graffiti on every sidewalk and shopwall, I was willing to agree with them.

But there in the deserted front hall of the guesthouse as I left that evening for dinner, undeniably saturated with normalcy as I was, I found myself avoiding King William's imperious eyes. Although reasonably confident that he would not dismount from his portrait to follow me down Antrim Road shrieking "papist!", I couldn't be sure he didn't suspect me of something. I thumbed my nose at the picture. There is a truculence to Belfast fantasies.

The presentation of fast food in the Six Counties is apparently as slow a process as it is in the Free State. It took the pleasant girl in a steamy fish & chips shop where I ordered a hamburger about fifteen minutes to combine what looked like a wet disk of peat with two deep-fried sponges and a cupful of seaweed. As she wrapped the greasy result in a few acres of newspaper, she asked a barrage of questions about America: Did I like Starsky and Hutch? Wasn't John Travolta smashing? Had I ever visited Hollywood? Weren't those neegers a terrible lot?

I asked her what made her think so poorly of "neegers".

"Ach, you see them on television. Do you like Kojak?"

"But Kojak is only a TV show," I protested. Another of America's indispensable exports. The fish & chips girl sniffed and seemed unconvinced.

"We've dreadful neegers here as well. You Yanks aren't the only ones."

Despairing of the argument, I left the shop with my newspaperful of grease. How could it be, with all the other plights and gripes of Belfast, that someone could afford the emotional expense of racist energy as well? Perhaps the only blacks seen on Antrim Road were the smack-dealers of Kojak and the frightened recruits of the British Army. On the train from Derry, I'd sat next to a social worker from London who lived in a predominantly black neighborhood. He had claimed that among every ten recruits from London, four were black.

With a diminishing appetite and a greasy bundle under my arm, I started walking down Antrim Road. A few blocks south of the fish & chips shop, unable to find anything like a park bench or a bus stop, I sat down on the curb across from what looked like a low-income housing project, spread my newspaper, and immediately regretted all the terrible things I'd said and thought about McDonald's hamburgers. There, smeared all over a week-old copy of the *Belfast Telegraph* was overwhelming evidence in favor of mass-hamburger production. What might not be accomplished for peace and concord here if only the inhabitants of Belfast could be offered a uniform fast-food as drab and unvariegated as the physical appearance of the city itself?

My contrivance of an assault on the hamburger was interrupted by the shouts of children across the street. In the courtyard of the housing project they had begun the construction of something that looked like a mountain of wood. It was hard to imagine where, in the grey stone streets that stretched monotonously in all directions, they could find so much lumber, but there they were, streaming out of doorways, alleys, and sidestreets like carpenter ants carrying plywood sheets, miles of half-round and quarterround, crates, bookshelves, nail-studded two-by-fours, and shattered furniture. Smaller kids stood at the top of the pile catching the pieces of timber tossed up by the stronger kids at the base, much the same way farm children in Kerry make haywinds.

As hesitantly as I'd approached the Black

Taxi dispatcher, I approached the industrious urchins. Their response was more childlike and innocent than his had been; they started to throw rocks.

Fortunately, however incoherent my cursing was, my voice didn't break, and the little monsters were immediately intrigued by my accent; they abandoned the woodpile to examine the Yankee curiosity which had accosted them.

"American, are ye?" This time, the question was a relief.

"Yeah!" Not yes, by any means. Two or three kids still had stones in their hands and I was trying as hard as I could to sound like Chuck Connors in *The Big Country.* "What're you fellas up to?"

The last few stones dropped and they all started screaming at once. Bonfires, bloody Brits, kick the bollix off 'em, whole bloody town tomorrah all over the place internment ye see.

Before long, the kids went back to their woodpile and I was walking up Antrim Road toward the guesthouse. The matronly landlady was waiting for me in the front hall and King William was staring over her shoulder at me as if he'd told her where I'd been. I was polite to both of them as she asked what I wanted for breakfast and what time I'd be leaving in the morning. Alone in my room that night, I said a prayer for Chuck Connors.

Internment, they'd said. I hadn't been watching the calendar, but I knew what the kids were talking about. Seven years earlier (tomorrow), British Prime Minister Heath had permitted the Stormont Government to resurrect the 1922 Special Powers Act, which provided for the indefinite internment of anybody suspected of just about anything, with neither legal counsel nor trial. Stormont had officially defended this action as a drastic attempt to neutralize Protestant as well as Catholic paramilitary groups, but to the majority of Ulster Catholics (as well as to human rights advocates all over the world), Internment quickly became a classical example of injustice.

On the first day of its implementation, nearly three hundred people were arrested—including three winos and a blind man—all but three of them Catholics and only seventy known to have any connections with the IRA. In the ensuing years, the anniversary of Internment had been marked with rioting and bloodshed in the northern cities. The kids had been constructing one of the hundres of bonfires that would dot the Catholic neighborhoods of Belfast tomorrow. Cathleen and Elizabeth would be at it again, as they had been since that day in 1169 when Strongbow landed with 200 knights and 1200 men-at-arms. Tomorrow fantasy would roar through the Belfast streets like a hurricane. I fell asleep.

Although I was determined not to break, I shuddered as I heard the groan of the cell-door bolt; the regular beating was about to resume, and, anticipating the pain, I drove my upper incisors into my lower lip. My eyes had long since been swollen shut, but I could hear the voice of the girl from the fish & chips shop soft and ominous in my ear: "Isn't John Travolta smashing?" I couldn't answer.

They had my arms pinned to the cell wall, the matronly landlady on my left, the Black Taxi dispatcher on my right. I could hear King Wiliam inhale sharply as he prepared to deliver another kick to my stomach. Whimpering and unable to form words, I was trying to say: "But I loved *Saturday Night Fever!* Viva Travolta! Please, I'll sign!"

Curled up like a fetus and suspicious that last night's hamburger had included diseased possum-flesh, I awoke. That morning I ate an invalid's breakfast of tea and cold toast, served by the landlady on a plate inscribed "frae bonnie Scotland".

King William was smirking when I left.

I wanted to see the Falls Road. Stretching

southwest from the City Center of Belfast, the Falls is the main street of a slum which contains the largest single concentration of Catholics in the Six Counties. Burnt-out and grey as the neighborhoods to the east, the lower Falls is, nonetheless, Cathleen Ni Houlihan's turf, and the appearance of plaster Madonnas in the rowhouse windows was as abrupt and startling as the sight of Confederate flags along the southernmost highways in Missouri. Foot patrols of British soldiers were everywhere, nervous-looking high school dropouts scanning rooftops and second-floor windows, stopping and searching pedestrians at random, avoiding eye-contact and going about their vague duties with an air of distaste. I was not, as my friends had told me I would be, astonished by the normalcy of things, but I was certainly astonished by the normalcy despite things. The detained residents of the neighborhood seemed numbed to the British presence, quietly handing over shopping bags for inspection, or lifting their arms to be frisked as if these things were merely another urban hassle, like traffic lights. The soldiers seemed to respond by being as impersonal as possible, oblivious even to the occasional jeers of bored little kids.

Falls Road is famous for sectarian violence. Although the atrocities had appreciably declined in frequency, the signs of a more violent period in Belfast history were everywhere. Husks of demolished buildings, bricked-up streetside windows, and tumorous-looking bunkers from which the soldiers watched passing traffic, these signs of the Ulster fighting looked like tattoos from an ancient, drunken night, all wearily ignored now.

Encircled by hurricane fences and cement-filled oildrums, the pubs looked like fortresses. The heavy oildrums once kept gelignite-filled cars from parking effectively close to the outside walls, and the chain-link prevented hand-thrown petrol and nail bombs from landing inside. But the anticipation of further violence indicated by the survival of these precautions seemed to have little effect on the pub trade. The residents of the Falls Road were cheerful as they surmounted the obstacles to a pint.

Since the gastric affront of the Antrim Road possumburger and the internal injuries inflicted by King William's feet were beginning to subside, I decided to risk a Guinness.

Soon I was standing in front of what looked like the entrance to one of the hurricane-fence cages, completely dumbfounded by the complicated latch which allowed access. A voice came from behind me.

"American, are ye?" No, Argentinian. I hadn't even opened my mouth!

The speaker was a pleasant-looking middle-aged man who introduced himself immediately, as if he'd been waiting for me to show up. "Tom Gavin. Pleasure." Opening the cage door with an ease that made me feel foolish, Tom held it wide and ushered me into the pub, ordering pints for both of us.

"And what's an American doing in Belfast, today of all days?"

I answered as honestly as I could, "Just seeing the sights, I guess."

"On the seventh anniversary of Internment. Daft." Not fully disagreeing with him, I couldn't come up with a defense for being in Belfast at all, so I started to ask questions about past anniversaries.

"They're all alike, I'd say. You'll see what they're like tonight, all right."

"But I won't be around tonight, Tom."

Will ye not be? Are ye busy somewhere else?"

There is a pleasant pattern to Celtic logic which will forever elude me. By the next round, Tom had decided not only that an American was not daft for being in Belfast on the seventh anniversary of Internment, but had implied that it was his party, that he would be hurt if I did not stay at his house that evening.

Tom Gavin was a prominent member in an

Michael Garvey

odd, claustral household of nearly a dozen single men. Except for Gippy, a retarded twenty-two year old and Liam, an unemployed secondary-school dropout, they all seemed to be middle-aged bachelors and widowers. Packed together in a diminutive two-floored row-house, they managed, with odd-jobs, pan-handling, and a few mild compromises with the local underworld, to pay the rent and to stock their tiny kitchen with bread, butter, eggs, milk and tea. A few years earlier, Liam told me, they had lived in a slightly larger building, but were displaced when a series of incen-diary bombs had left most of their block in ruins.

Of the thousand instances I had so far en-countered in Ireland, the hospitality of that strange Falls Road community was by far the most generous. As Tom, Liam, Gippy and I sat with ritual formality in the parlor, Felix, a pleasantly officious roommate questioned us thoroughly about eggs:

"First you, Mike. Softboiled, is it? How de ye mean soft? The yolk liquidy-like? Good. Now you, Gip, two minutes, is it? Now Tom, hard-like-a-stone, I know . . . " Some passion for intricacy subsists, I'm convinced, in the Irish unconscious. The patient monk responsible for the filigree which rims the Ardagh Chalice

122

gave to that passion aesthetic form, but that afternoon in Belfast, in the offering of soft-boiled eggs, Felix transformed it to genius. If hospitality is an artform, the Irish are masters; the two pieces of toast, the softboiled egg and the cup of tea Felix served made up one of the most delicious meals of my life.

We ate in comfortable silence, occasionally punctuated by brief comments on Felix's fine cooking and, of course, by "the noise."

It was an amazing parlor. Displayed on the mantlepiece above a coal-burning, cast-iron fireplace were the sorts of knick knacks you would expect to see in a spinster's house. Incongruously feminine baubles: a miniature clipper-ship crafted entirely of seashells, a felt-covered statue of a cocker spaniel with large, pleading, humanoid eyes, a pincushion of red velvet, and a delicate Waterford vase containing an arrangement of plastic lilies. Above these and surrounded by a huge rococo frame, hung a saccharine depiction of the Sacred Heart. Into the bottom of the frame, close to the congealing blood which flowed with almost photographic realism from the ruptured ventricles, someone had tucked two postcards of girly cartoons.

After tea, we sat smoking cigarettes and listening to Felix, who by his proprietary tones in

describing them, gave the impression that he
had invented the political and sectarian fric-
tions which ravaged Belfast. As the attentions
of the others wandered (it was apparent that
they were long familiar with his analysis of the
situation), I became the primary target of his
rhetoric.

"Why does someone in authority not go to
the Brits and say: Now come here. You've
maintained your presence on this island for
eight hundred years through nothing but force
of arms. Why do ye not leave, now?"

I couldn't think of an answer. There was
none. Triumphant in the consequent pause,
Felix sighed and leaned back in his chair, as if
something had been settled.

During that recent period of our own
history, when inner-city ghettos all over the
North American continent were erupting what
government euphuists call "urban unrest",
Julius Lester told an instructive story. Cleve-
land policemen were enforcing a curfew in an
area of the city which had been troubled by
sniper fire. Probably reluctant to stay inside
on a hot night, a little kid protested to one of the
cops: It's not us they're shooting at. It's you.
The peace-keeping pretensions of the British
Army, at least it seemed to me, in the Falls
Road area of Belfast, eventually confront that

sort of awareness. If there is a glimmering of solidarity among the right wing Republicans, the hard-core Provos, the socialist Sinn Feiners, the burnt-out, war-weary and understandably apathetic welfare recipients, it's expressed in the recurring graffito: Brits Out. Peace In.

But clustered around that reasonable aspiration is a hopeless confusion of method and motive. A principal tributary of the Internment Day Parade formed that evening in an intersection close to the bachelors' house. Among the crowd, which swarmed along the Falls a good kilometer and a half, from Albert Street to Grosvernor Road, were members of The Relatives Action Committee, Sinn Fein organizers, representatives of the Belfast Branch of the Communist Party (Leninists) and a convent-school marching band. Band members quarreled and squealed, insincerely smiling for their parents' Instamatics and ignoring the frustrated band director as well as the inappropriately camouflaged British Army helicopters which roared above the street.

And there were many, many drunks. Although it was to commemorate a grim event and a serious purpose, the parade seemed triumphal and celebratory; the girls band played "A Nation Once Again," the tricolor fluttered everywhere, old men marched at attention, and pram-pushing housewives screamed at unruly children all the way to Casement Park where thousands of people had already gathered.

No matter how complex, whether inflicted by institution or directionless passion, the agony of Belfast's poor is genuine and intense. Everyone has suffered a loss—a sense of order, a kneecap, an uncle or a spouse—and none of these is a trivial thing. But silhouetted against the fearful immensity of such losses, the baroque oratory and sentimental gesture of the Casement Park rally seemed a desecration of sacred possibility. Emotions were explosive and language correspondingly excessive. The abused and rebellious prisoners of H Block, that notorious wing of the Long Kesh Prison, were frequently referred to as "the cream of Irish manhood," a status determined, one orator screamed, by resistance of "the Saxon Huns." A weeping old woman, the mother of a recently imprisoned H Block victim, was sympathetically escorted from the speakers' platform, unable to finish her speech. Applause was so thunderous the helicopters of the queen could no longer be heard, but the collective enthusiasm seemed doomed to the football game-Barry Fitzgerald movie level. Furious and exhilarated, fully prepared by design or coincidence, the crowd was ready for the riot to begin.

During the rally the children of Belfast had continued to dismantle the slums for bonfire fuel. By sundown, every wide place in Falls Road was aflame; above Antrim Road there was an impermeable haze of black smoke from the car tires which had been tossed on the coals. Children were rolling tires down the Falls, too, and soon the bonfires turned a deeper orange and issued a blacker smoke, like the factory chimneys of Gary, Indiana. Pungent, rubbery smoke, carried by a mild southerly breeze drifted into the bachelors' strange parlor, where Liam, Gippy and I left Felix and Tom coughing and arguing.

We stood in the doorway to watch the riot.

A curious theory of counterinsurgency had earlier that month prompted Her Majesty's forces to remove the toilet from Belfast's Sinn Fein headquarters during a routine and purposeless raid. The response of the British to the Internment disturbances that night was equally bewildering. Foot patrols were assigned to advance along Falls Road until they encountered rock-throwing mobs and retreated under a hail of stones. Saracen tanks, peppering everything everywhere with rubber bullets, were also deployed. These would move through the streets crushing bonfires and barricades, pelted from windows, doorways, alleys and parked cars with anything small enough to be thrown. For insurgents and counterinsurgents alike, the work of violence was carried on in a strange, ritualistic way, as if both sides were halfheartedly going through the motions.

When the paint store in the next block went off like a bomb, Liam winced and continued to describe a Charles Bronson movie about a jailbreak; Gippy squealed with delight, as if it had been a firecracker; Tom, slightly drunk and scratching his belly, emerged from the parlor and asked what all the commotion was about. "Paint store's gone off," simple Gippy seemed proud, as if he'd accomplished something. Tom shrugged and said, "Fuck me, anyhow." Everyone else in the house was sleeping, or trying to sleep.

And that was that.

The parlor filled early next morning with grumpy and reluctantly awakening boarders; squinting through the soot at the television set, they packed their lunches and slurped their tea, quarreling about the accuracy of the local news reports which punctuated the Roadrunner cartoons.

In the streets outside, Falls' natives were going to work, pointedly ignoring the resumption of the soldiers' patrols. The weird confederations of children who had stoked last night's bonfires were now shovelling up the embers and clearing the streets.

Having thanked Tom, Liam, Felix, Gippy and the others, I said goodbye and started for the City Center to find a Dublin-bound train. Three times between their house and Divis Street, I, with other randomly chosen pedestrians, was frisked by bored Englishmen. At the Central Railway Station, after my final Ulster frisk, I bought a newspaper and discovered that the Falls Road chaos had achieved page 2. Football scores filled the front page.

The coffee shop of the station was packed with well-dressed and prosperous looking people; I felt nervous, out of place, and not quite confident that my fly was zipped up. People were looking at me strangely. All of these suspicions were exacerbated by that frail, stunned feeling which usually follows a sleepless night, and eventually I dismissed my discomfort as a spasm of paranoia. But then the waitress seemed unnecessarily icy when she brought my coffee, and the ticket vendor ignored my open palm, clattering my change on the countertop, and the man in the seat opposite mine on the train walled off all attempts at small talk with the *Irish Times*. As mild paranoia threatened to become panic, I tried to calm myself by pretending to sleep and by concentrating on the Charles Bronson movie which had so impressed Liam that he had overlooked an exploding building while describing it.

At Connoly Station, Dublin, the uneasiness remained unrelenting, and my quick walk to sanctuary at a bed & breakfast house was excruciating. When I entered the bathroom to take a shower, the face which stared back at me from the mirror made me jump. It was pitch-black from the bonfire soot.

State O'Chassis

*b*IS SOCIOLOGICAL STUDIES, Father
Andrew Greeley announced, have led him to
believe that societal oppression has an ugly
afterlife, like an inadequately removed tumor.
Second class citizens, he says, tend to absorb
the unjust attitudes of the ruling class towards
them; perversely, they attempt to confront
stereotypes by enfleshing them, a tension
which results in an obsessive self-loathing.
American Catholics, for instance, now at least
a couple of generations away from any real
(specific?) oppression, must regard their
Church in much the same way that WASPs for-
merly did, as oppressive, narrowminded, anti-
intellectual, and sexhating. I think Father
Greeley has something there.

At Notre Dame, for example, an Irish American who loves his ancestry is indirectly required to display its peculiar ethnic charisms
(or at least those things which he has been led
to believe are ethnic charisms): drunkenness,
sloth, fear of the opposite sex, gloom, and a
cosmology of guilt as pervasive as atmospheric
pressure. While I was there I heard an otherwise sensible woman describe a mutual ac-
quaintance who was Irish, sober, hardwork-
ing, and generally optimistic: "He doesn't

131

drink; he's always happy, and he gets things done. Sometimes I think he's not really Irish."

The poor man. If he didn't grow depressed or nervous enough to periodically drink himself senseless, if he enjoyed his work so much that he did it very well, if he found the circumstances of his life pleasant and was happy with them, how could he be Irish? What would have been praise for a Swede, a black, a German, or a Briton, became for him a disturbing flaw, a hint that something had gone wrong somewhere. As far as I know, my friend is now leading a happy, healthy, productive life, married to a woman he loves, raising children who love them both very much, doing good things in a world with which he is at peace. A real tragedy.

Nevertheless, I sympathize with the attempt to stereotype Irish Catholics, and I would be happy to do so if I could only put my finger on what they have in common. So far, I understand that the home of the Irish is a lovely, intricate, and compact island in the North Sea, that hospitality and courtesy (whether deeply rooted or not) seems to proliferate there, and that I don't understand anything else about them at all.

But no book about Ireland would be complete without at least one of the stereotypes that

Father Greeley so justifiably condemns, and this is mine:

Irish hamburgers are abominations.

The Irish simply do not know how to make hamburgers. They have never known how to make hamburgers. They may never know how to make hamburgers. Everything, so professors of philosophy have told me, needs a significant opposite. There is a tavern in Rock Island, Illinois, where you can find the Platonic form of The Hamburger. In Rock Island, you can buy a thing that spills over with what it is and has, generously being everything that a hamburger is, everything that a hamburger could possibly be: a Hamburger accountably Hamburgering. And anywhere in Ireland, especially where hamburgers are advertised, you will find the hamburger's significant opposite: a thing which not only is not a hamburger, but which actively and maliciously un-hamburgers.

McDonald's' corporate strategists were quick to detect and exploit this massive Irish incapacity, and like capitalists everywhere, they rushed in to occupy a terrain which might have been more charitably approached. Their grip on the Irish gastronomic imagination is now lethal. But what might have been accomplished against the decline of Western Civilization by a decent Rock Island hamburger chef with a modicum of missionary zeal?

Perhaps there is a variation of the selfloathing dynamic which Father Greeley has observed at the heart of the Irish Hamburger Problem. If the Yanks are capable of producing something as odious as the Big Mac, the reasoning may go, we, the Irish, will not be outdone. We will make something worse. (Come to think of it, there might be something like this going on with the arms race and the urge to make ever more destructive toys for undersexed Pentagon officials, but that's another matter altogether.)

I myself fell victim to this lunatic reasoning one night in Dublin. I was standing in line at a hamburger place watching the fascinating process by which fat and gristle become hard to identify while remaining oddly associable with the Animal Kingdom. The man at the grill asked me what I would like on my hamburger, and I told him curry sauce. If he was capable of the Yankee-hamburger-loathing which engendered these threatening disks, I was capable of transforming them into something even worse with the simple addition of curry sauce. We had both, obviously, gone slightly mad.

After a few moments of snarling and confused negotiation, we agreed on a recipe and named the result the Iowaburger. Triumphant and convinced I'd come up with a worse hamburger than any Irishman could dream of, I carried my prize out of the place, sat down on the concrete stoop of the Georgian house next door, spread the customary four acres of greasy newspaper, and began to eat.

The sidewalk in front of the stoop was aswarm with Dublin pedestrians. It was getting late, and the pubs, dancehalls, theatres, sodality meetings and secondshift jobs were releasing night-people by the thousands. The steps of the building were drenched in the lonely fluorescence of the blue hamburger sign, and people seemed to be glaring at me with sympathy. For the sad light I was sitting in, for the fact that I must now try to eat an Iowaburger, or perhaps for the fact that I seemed to have nothing more urgent to do than to sit alone on the steps with my greasy meal, watching them watch me. It was delightful.

An old priest weaved up the sidewalk and came to an uncertain halt in front of the place. Slightly drunk, overweight and bald, he swayed there, regarding me solemnly through unfocused and heavy-lidded eyes, as if we were about to begin an uncomfortable face-to-face confession.

"Yer name, Son?"

Michael Garvey

I told him.

"From these parts, are ye?"

"From Iowa, Father, in America."

"I-o-way. I know about I-o-way, I do." That made me uneasy. I couldn't tell if he meant that I shouldn't tell him any more about Iowa or that he knew many terrible things for which Iowa was responsible and that he would now begin to correct them, starting with me. Like so many drunks, he seemed convinced that his last statement had enormous significance, and he watched me with odd confidence that I would soon understand. Not sure of the polite thing to do, I bit into a potato chip, still watching him with an attentive expression. Finally he spoke again.

"What is that thing yer eatin', Son?"

"An Iowaburger. Wanna bite?"

"I don't mind." Half the burger disappeared into his mouth while he inhaled slightly, the grease, curry, and the edges of his lips making an alarming, percolative noise. He winced at the curry.

"What do you call that again?"

"An Iowaburger, Father."

"Poisonous . . . I must be leaving you now, Son. Goodnight, and bless ye."

With inebriated grace, he bowed vaguely, turned, and began to leave, but hesitated, as if he'd forgotten something.

"An I-o-wayburger, was it?"

"It was, Father." I might have told him of a familial tragedy, his expression was so genuinely compassionate. A thing so terrible, he seemed to be thinking, could not be my fault.

"Do ye not know of McDonald's Hamburger Restaurant in Grafton Street, Son?" he asked kindly.

"I do, Father."

The old man signed, "Poisonous as well, I suppose. I really must leave ye now, Son. Here are the lads ye were waiting for." Unaware that I'd been waiting for anyone, I looked away from the retreating priest to find that "the lads" were a pair of adolescent males with long, greasy hair, shining vinyl jackets and quick, nervous movements. They flanked me on the steps like old friends.

"Fine evening, isn't it?" With that introduction, uttered in a barely penetrable Ulster accent, there began a litany of inane questions about my travels and opinions, neither of which seemed sincerely to interest the new arrivals. They glanced over their shoulders as they spoke. I was getting confused.

"American, are ye?" one of them asked.

"No. I'm from Yugoslavia." Both of them laughed with enthusiasm disproportionate to the joke, and the litany continued, suddenly abbreviated by the quiet observation of the one on my left, "Here' re the peelers now."

On the sidewalk in front of us, a small blue sedan had pulled up, disgorging two awkward looking but well-dressed men, cleancut and cleareyed as Air Force cadets. "The lads" stood up quickly, as if they had expected the confrontation.

I can't think of any convincing reason why Ireland shouldn't have plainclothes policemen, but their appearance at that moment in the blue light of the hamburger sign, so immediately following the bewildering interviews with the drunken priest and the two Ulster teenagers, seemed metaphysically inappropriate. If the two Ulstermen had been escaped ax-murderers intent on the intricate mutilation of a luckless Yank, the arrival of the gardai would not have been less disquieting. I disliked them from the start.

Ignoring me and my Iowaburger, they began to question the Ulster lads, asking names, residences, reasons for being there, places of employment, and where they had been that evening. One cop suddenly turned to me. "And who's this gentleman with you?"

There was something disconcerting about the policeman's evident annoyance at my American accent. Hostile and unconvinced, he seemed to think I was an impudent Dubliner with a talent for mimicry.

"American, are ye?" No, Flatfoot, Damascene. Philip Marlowe would have said something like that, blowing cigarette smoke into the guy's face and adding something like: Did that ear for detail get you taken off the parking violation squad? Although tempted to use the Chandlerism, I remembered that the Dublin police I'd so far encountered hadn't displayed extraordinary fascination with verbal recreation or the exercise of the ironic.

"Yes, I'm an American."

"Have ye any identification? Passport? Anything?"

"I'll show you mine if you'll show me yours." I'd remembered that from a detective movie. Deeply impressed by my wit and bravery (and emboldened by the fact that he didn't punch me out), I took a long time deciphering, or trying to, the incomprehensible piece of official-looking paper he handed me.

The cop took my passport and began to transcribe everything written there, snapping question after question as he did so. How long had I been in Ireland? Who did I know in Dublin? Where had I been that evening? How long had I known these two? Where was I living at the moment? Then suddenly my passport was returned with the suggestion that I get lost.

"But I haven't finished, yet."

Finished what?"

"My Iowaburger."

One of the Ulstermen asked what an Iowa-burger was, and I began to explain. The police told us both to shut up, transforming me into (or perhaps confirming me as) an ugly American. If we weren't being arrested, and if we weren't charged with any crime, wasn't there some Irish law which protected us from all this?

"You Yanks," the second cop pointed out, "are cute ones. All the answers, haven't you?" But I'd only been asking questions.

"Feck 'em," the first cop suggested to the second. "We'll be off, now, but don't ye be tryin' anything cute, you." And they were gone.

The lads from Ulster cheerfully flashed to the angry, departing police that gesture which in the late sixties in America meant "peace," but which in Ireland, as I mentioned earlier, means something else.

To this day, I don't know why we were all questioned. The Ulstermen, perhaps melodramatically, claimed that anyone from the North was treated that way by the Dublin police, and that their only crime that evening had been to drink at a Republican bar. "The peelers assume we're carryin' bombs and drugs and feck all, only because we're from Derry. This goes on all the time," one of them said, adding that if I hadn't been there, they would surely have spent the night in jail without charge.

He may have been lying through his teeth; the two of them may have kicked an old woman to death that night just for squeaks, and my presence in front of the hamburger place may have been a genuine obstruction of justice. Whatever engendered the entire incident, it was the only unpleasant occurrence during my stay in the Free State.

That night the same policemen visited my bed & breakfast to confirm, I suppose, the truth of my claim to be staying there. "Just routine," they assured my frightened land-lady, who viewed me for the rest of my stay in Dublin with great interest and, I think, mild distrust. I reveled in the mystery which now surrounded me and hoped that the pretty German girl down the hall thought I was a gangster or a C.I.A. agent.

tHE DUBLIN GUARDS were hard at it, and nobody knew what they were doing. I think that they themselves were unsure of their mission, but they went about its execution with mysterious intensity, three of them standing in the middle of O'Connell Street, flagging down random automobiles and beaming flashlights into the interiors. Their manner seemed, as always, distant, polite, and taciturn; none of the drivers seemed particularly upset by the halfhearted searches, as if the guards' odd curiosity about incoming Dublin traffic were an unquestioned local custom.

I was leaning against a parking meter, watching the proceedings, when I noticed a man leaning against another parking meter a few yards up the street. He seemed to be watching me.

After a few minutes of this, I began to feel as silly as the guards, so I nodded to him, and he spoke.

"Grand evenin'."

"Sure is. What do you think they're looking for?"

"Don't ye worry about what they're lookin' for. They'll find it soon enough."

"But isn't this an unusual thing? I mean look

at them; stopping cars and searching them
without telling anybody what they're looking
for, or why they're looking in that particular
car."

"They've their reasons, I'd say." He seemed
annoyed by the question.

"Do you think they'd tell me if I asked them?
Would they mind?"

His annoyance increased visibly.

"Yer a Yank, are ye not?"

"I am." (After a week in Dublin, I'd forgotten the word "yes".)

"Now, I don't claim to know a great deal
about American custom, sir," (his tone was, to
put it mildly, sarcastic) "but in this country,
and especially in this city, we're not in the
habit of preventin' our guards from the per-
formance of their duties."

"But I didn't say anything about that at all. I
was just wondering *why* they're searching
cars. For all I know, they might have the best
reasons in the world; aren't you curious?"

"Oh, they have their reasons, and ye may be
sure of that. Don't dispute the integrity of the
Dublin guards. Ye will find no finer. Anywhere."

The guards continued to flag down and
search the cars, occasionally muttering into
their walky-talkies. The man at the parking

meter turned his attention from me to the street, and watched the inquisitive police with admiration all over his face. "Sound lads," he said, softly and with wonder.

I approached the nearest guard, and as I did so, the man at the meter rushed forward to intervene, like an attentive bartender who notices a brawl in its embryonic stages. The man shouldered me out of the way with startling suddenness, speaking loudly to the guard before I could open my mouth.

"Excuse me! Guard! Excuse me!" The guard touched his cap and walked over to us.

The man spoke with exaggerated politeness, as if he were a little boy and the guard were a famous war hero. "Grand evenin' isn't it?" How's the work?" The guard touched his hat again and smiled vaguely.

"Thanks very much. Excuse me." He turned, spoke into his walky-talky, and returned to the center of the street.

This seemed to satisfy the man at the meter, and he turned back to me in triumph, as if the whole mystery had been explained. "Didn't I tell ye? Didn't I? No finer, anywhere."

I gave up.

The pubs were closing and the man at the meter invited me back to his house for tea. At a fish and chips stop we picked up a couple of greasy newspaper bundles and walked away from the town center into a dingier neighborhood, where, after a labyrinthine journey through alleys and courtyards, we came to his back door. He turned to me with his index finger pressed against his lips. "It's the mother," he whispered. "She's asleep; we must be quiet now."

Guilt was a palpable force in the hushed, dim kitchen, where we spread our grease-sodden newspapers beneath the effeminate gaze of the Sacred Heart. "The Mother" was everywhere in the house, it seemed, and for fear of waking her, we kept our voices low.

"She's been ill for some time now, de ye see," the man said quietly, "and I think she's a bit uneasy in her sleep." From some dark corner, he produced bottles of Harp lager, passing one to me and seeming to forget the water which he'd placed on the stove to boil. We ate and drank for a minute in monastic silence.

Suddenly he spoke. "Let me show you something."

"By all means."

He disappeared for a few moments and returned with a long, flat box, bulging and wrapped with rubber bands. Photographs.

"Who would ye say that is." It was a young man smiling.

"It looks like yourself." He beamed.

"And what do ye think of this one?" A pretty girl in a bathing suit.

"Your girlfriend?" He laughed loudly, agreeing, and slapped my shoulder before remembering "The Mother"; he grew gloomy and worried again.

"She's a fine one all right," he whispered, "and we're to be married soon, only I've to take care of the mother first." He picked up the photograph of the girl and smiled into it for a while. As if he were speaking to himself, he said, "She's teaching in Wicklow at the moment."

"Your girl?" He seemed startled, and looked from the photograph to me with a blank stare.

"Ah. That's right. Wicklow." We were silent a few more moments. "Here. Let me show you something."

He led me from the kitchen to a small, dark parlor, telling me to stand still in one spot. He walked over to a light switch and flicked it, and every light in the room seemed to focus on a gigantic portrait of a beautiful young woman. The Mother, he explained, when she was much younger. There was also a piano in the room, and stacks of classical sheet music; when she was younger the Mother had been an accomplished classical pianist. He showed me a trophy case jammed with awards from musical societies and letters from famous people, thanking her for this recital or that composition. We both stared at the portrait until his eyes began to fill with tears. I was uncomfortable, so I coughed and said, "It's very beautiful."

His tone was fierce, but his voice trembled. "Yer shaggin' right about that. She's a great one, she is." We returned to the kitchen and spoke more about his girlfriend, whom he would marry when the Mother died, and at midnight I left, warned by the sad man not to speak ill of the Dublin guards.

It occurred to me on the way back to the town center that the man and I had not exchanged names.

Michael Garvey

IT WAS my last day in Dublin, and a miscalculation of the train schedule gave me an extra two hours to kill. I entered a crowded pub near Connolly Station seconds before Holy Hour. With the beginning of the hour, the exuberant chatter of the place dropped sharply in volume, and the tone of the jokes and stories shifted from the declamatory and heroic to the muted and conspiratorial. The shades were pulled down quickly and in the newly dimmed light and the guilt-tinged hush of the place, the pale eye of the television set above the bar drew increased attention. With a monotonous flute playing softly in the background, Jane Fonda, dressed like a medieval queen (well, like a Southern Californian's notion of a medieval queen) was riding a black stallion on a bright and sandy beach.

Jane Fonda . . . If you ever grow bored enough to make a list of her many talents, be sure to exclude historical scholarship. I remember her passionate and well-meaning objection to the American presence in Vietnam a few years ago, phrased in a striking rhetorical question. How, she asked, would we Americans feel if some other country, like France, had become involved in our revolution? That was on the Dick Cavett Show, which was probably aired, among many other places, in Lafayette, Indiana. In the awkward silence which preceded the jeers, many of us who agreed with her objections became painfully aware that here was another stunningly attractive spokesperson we could do without.

At least Vanessa Redgrave has the sense to utter silly declaratives instead of damaging rhetorical questions.

Although my credentials as a historican are not much more impressive than Ms. Fonda's, I had several times during that Irish visit felt moved to ask a similarly vulnerable question: What single institution in history has ever been responsible for more human suffering, social indignity and moral ruin than the British Empire?

The blue light of the television set seemed to be on the verge of disclosing a terrible answer as the wealthy activist continued her gallop on the beach past the dulled eyes of roughly four dozen silenced Dubliners. A rough beast was slouching our way, all right.

As if he were thinking the same sorts of thoughts, the barman threw a wet rag against the control panel of the TV set; horse, rider, and beach vanished and the spell was broken. People began to talk freely again, released a few moments from the deleterious onslaught of bottomless consumerism, those spicy invitations to buy everything imaginable.

A cheerful young woman, spastic and evidently braindamaged, made her difficult way along the bar, thumping the tweed backs of the drinkers for no obvious reason. Many of the men engaged her in affectionate but mocking conversation. Their eyes filled with glee when she had particular trouble with a word and they eagerly supplied her with lists of more complicated challenges to her crippled phonetics. Apparently unconscious of their half-hearted cruelty, she played the game happily as a handful of other patrons mimed her crazy motions in silence behind her back. All of this deeply entertained the barman who grinned savagely as he nodded encouragement at her and winked approval at her audience.

Older demons than seductively televised capitalism haunted this town. I finished my pint and returned to the grey streets outside.

The shrieks and clatters of Connolly Station evaporated the depressing memory of the bar and made me more anxious than ever to get out of Dublin. Everybody in the place was sprinting for the trains, none of which showed any inclination to move. I felt like sprinting myself, but had no idea of the appropriate train to choose for a goal. Not far from where I stood, and similarly immobile, an angry young man stood in the center of what looked like a Boy Scout supply dump. He wearily assembled the four tons of camping gear, hoisted it onto his shoulders with a gasp, walked about fifteen feet, dropped it to the floor, cursed quietly, regathered his strength, and assembled the gear again. I watched this process for a few cycles before asking him if I could give him a hand, and he was elaborately grateful.

"Unreasonably kind of ye, Lad. What part of America are ye from?"

"Iowa. Out in the middle."

"I've always wanted to go there."

"Iowa?"

"And New York, as well." What a polite thing to say about my state! "And where is it yer goin' to?"

"Tralee, I hope."

"Mercifull Hour!" (Merciful Hour?) "I'm bound that way myself." Nick O'Rourke, as he introduced himself, worked at a candy factory in Dublin; having earned a week-long vacation, he had agreed to rendezvous with some friends at a campsite west of Dingle. "But what the gobshites neglected to tell me was that they wanted me to collect all their bloody gear as well!" This task, he told me, had been made

triply difficult by a drinking episode last night.
Nick's inebriation had been intense enough to
necessitate his vomiting from a third-floor
window, but pleasant and irrevocable enough
to make him unconscious of the fact that in
order to get rid of the night's undigested
porter, he had leaned heavily against a steam
heat radiator in excellent working condition.
He had sustained severe burns on his thighs.

But despite what must have been a soul-
searing hangover and an inability to move his
legs unaided by blasphemy, Nick seemed in
high holiday spirits as we approached the
Cork-bound train. He was, he explained, leaving Dublin for the first time in his life.

The train was like a monstrous sociological
experiment, poorly conceived by behavioral
psychologists to learn more about human
responses to claustrophobia and emotional
stress. Busy and alarming as mudwasps,
swarms of young people were insulting the
cars with bright orange backpacks; nylon was
hissing against denim, and in the swirl of
smoke, noise, and disagreement, German folk
music enthusiasts and stoned North American
university students formed a vague, implaca-
ble, amorphous threat to everything that was
good. Panicky conductors were battling the

mob swell, begging insolent bicyclists to remove their twelve-speed racers from the aisles
as two Dominican nuns, tightlipped, furious,
and immobile as penguins waited with exaggerated patience to escape the smoking section. We tourists were by far the predominant
cargo, but several young Irish women, seem-
ingly oblivious to the anarchy, were crowding
about the small tables flanking the car.
Spreading movie magazines, chocolates, cigarette packages, handbags and small bottles
of fingernail polish across every available
horizontal surface, they chatted happily about
boring clerical work and insensitive boy-
friends, about the frenzy and ennui of Dublin
life and the calm joys of the Western countryside. All the wretched conductors could bring
to the hysteria was pleading: "Ladies and
Gents! Please! Please now!"—the whimpering
of a dying order, the death throes of reason
and manners as Ireland sank in the secular
bog.

The train jerked, shuddered, and began to
move quietly in the direction of Los Angeles.
Nick and I pushed into the crowd with bags
and curses. The nuns vanished into the blue
smoke.

The train emptied gradually as it moved
westward, sprinkling the flat, grassy midlands

with tourists, Deutschmarks and American Express traveler's checks; herds of Bostonians disembarked at each Tipperary stop, benevolently raiding various family reunions, weddings and burials; nearly all the Germans left the train at Mallow, heading for the Gaeltachts and folk music in the Southwest. Somewhere in Limerick, Nick had fallen into a feverish and moaning sleep, and by the time we reached the Kerry border the conductor had filled the seats across from us with the two Dominican nuns and their baggage.

The moods of Sister Reginald and Felicitas were clearly improved by the departure of the noisy, smoky crowd, and they chatted freely as Nick snored. Sr. Felicitas, the younger of the two, seemed to think that everything in the world was a grand thing to be or see or do or know. It was a grand thing that I was American. Ireland was grand, Dublin was grand, Listowel, where she and Sr. Reginald were going to visit with Sr. Reginald's family, was grand. It was grand that Nick could sleep so soundly despite the noise of the train, grand that I was going to Tralee, grand that I would be hitchhiking from there to Dingle. It was grand that I was traveling, grand that I had seen Dublin, and grand that I had met Nick. Sr. Reginald, although not seeming to be in complete disagreement with Sr. Felicitas about that cheerful cosmology, was nonetheless more cautious about life; as Sr. Felicitas wound down her litany of life's grandeur, the older nun grunted and pointed to Nick. "Yer man's returning, I think."

As if on cue, Nick, his eyes clenched shut and his right foot driving into Sr. Reginald's right knee, began a long and apparently painful stretch. His yawn was fierce and passionate, emphasized unbearably by the clear enunciation of a bizarre sentence concerning theology, hatred, and a complicated sexual act. He broke the sentence sharply in the middle of the concluding prepositional phrase, having opened his eyes and seen his outraged audience.

"Oh. Sister. Sorry."

Silence. I became fascinated by the green blur of the passing hedge outside.

Nick nudged me. Guilt, embarrassment, defiance, humor, panic and pleading warred for predominance in his facial expression. It looked like an emotional map of Ireland.

"Did I fall asleep, Mick, did I?"

That's right, Nick. The important thing is that you fell asleep. There aren't two completely freaked out nuns across the seat from you. You didn't just utter a statement which they believe marks you as an emergency candidate for exorcism, and they won't go to confession tonight for having overheard it. Yes, you must have fallen asleep, Nick.

"I guess you did."

"Well, then. I'll be . . . "

"This is Sr. Reginald and this is Sr. Felicitas. They're on their way to Listowel. We were just talking." What an inane thing to include.

"Oh," Nick was frantic and desperately enthusiastic. "Listowel? Isn't that a grand thing?"

Sr. Felicitas' eyes lit up, and she agreed loudly. She and Nick began to chatter uncomfortably about how grand things were. I made a few attempts to engage Sr. Reginald in further conversation but she was silent and glared at the three of us for the rest of the journey.

It was an unusually clear day in Kerry, and from a beach near Dingle I saw Skellig Michael looming, almost thirty miles out. Looming is about the only thing that Skellig Michael can do these days; it hasn't been inhabited for centuries. It rises steeply and high from the Atlantic like an excessively drawn Walt Disney conception, and people have told me that no other place on earth is as tranquil in fair weather nor terrifying in foul. At the summit of the rock, there is an ancient and well preserved monastic ruin, accessible by helicopter on a clear day, and built, like so many others, on a site where the Druids once worshiped. Some people believe that Skellig Michael was the object of St. Brendan's mystical voyage, that it was the only place in Europe untouched by the Black Death, that attacks by the Norsemen invariably failed there.

Only gannets live there now. About a hundred yards from the beach, out beyond the incoming breakers, the sea was churning with them, weird ocean-buzzards which drop like guided missiles from astounding heights to swallow mackarel and to bob stupidly on the surface while they digest. Every fisherman in the area has a story (the story) about a gannet sinking his own boat, or a friend's. Nevertheless, the relationship between fishermen and gannets seems to be a friendly one.

Off to my right, I saw a huge promontory of land where Cromwell once drove and disarmed three hundred papists and then gave the order for them to be slaughtered and thrown into the sea. People in Kinard speak of the event as if they witnessed it. That civilized man, Edmund Spenser, who invented one of the most engaging and complex sonnet forms in

English verse, was one of Cromwell's staff that day, and helped carry out the order.

Cresting one of the breakers, a bright red Coca-Cola can attempted to land on the Kerry beach. It may have been the large amount of coffee I'd drunk that morning or the large amount of porter I'd drunk the night before. It may have been the condescension of an Irish-American visitor, independent of the island but jealously defending a threatened preconception of something ancient and pure, and it may have been ordinary boredom; but at that moment, it seemed essential that the Coca-Cola can not touch Irish soul. I scooped up a handful of gravel and took up the fight for old Ireland, throwing the pebbles with a childish and lunatic enthusiasm until the coke can sank beneath the incoming waves.

It probably washed up a few hours later, anyway.

MR. TIMOTHY McPHEE, although a devoted and unashamed Pioneer, did not look much like a teetotaler. His slow-moving, opthalmic eyes were bloodshot and brooding, much like the eyes of a man who had drunk heavily the night before. Furthermore, the waistband of his powder-blue leisure suit bulged uncomfortably with what would, on a drinking man, have been a beerbelly. His wife Molly sat beside him on the front seat, half-turned toward me, nervously stroking her elaborate and swollen coiffure and giggling loudly at my John Wayne imitations. I liked them.

The McPhees were childless, middleaged, affluent, and, I think, a little lonely that afternoon. With a shy introductory confession that they were often suspicious of hitchhikers, they had picked me up on the road leading north from Sligo, about twenty miles from their destination, the Donegal resort town, Bundoran.

Their home was Prehen, a comfortable suburb of Derry, and the harshness of their Ulster accents seemed strange after the softer speech of Kerry, Limerick, Clare, Galway and Sligo, those counties through which I'd ascended toward Donegal. Unlike the natives of those

counties, the McPhees had a word for "yes."
"Aye," they would say, making the association
between their accent and that of Scotland
surer and stronger. Aye, they said, they had
been to Galway for the races, but there was no
room for them in the hotels there. There was
something sad about their disappointed return
to Derry, and they seemed resigned to the failure of their attempt to have fun, as if their
whole life together had been a series of such
failures. From their enthusiasm to speak to me
about anything except their vacation, I gathered that their stopping for a hitchhiker was its
high point. They would probably write to their
relatives in America and England about the
young American they'd picked up; all the
things he'd said, all the things they'd said to
him.

Something about their cautious friendliness
and innocent reluctance to speak of themselves made me think that their stopping for me
(or for any other hitchhiker) required impressive amounts of courage and charity.

"We're only going to Bundoran," said Mr.
McPhee, long after we had established that
destination, as if he were frantically groping
for something new to say. "We've been down
to Galway for the races, only they hadn't a
room in the town but it's a grand thing to be

traveling like this all the same, I think." He repeated that statement a dozen times in twenty miles, Mrs. McPhee continued her loud giggling and sideways glances at her taciturn husband, and I, like an idiot, continued to imitate John Wayne. In this confusing manner, we entered the town of Bundoran.

Mr. McPhee regarded the recurrent Bed and Breakfast signs with suspicion. "I wonder would they have room at all?" he kept muttering, as if the signs were lying to us. Mrs. McPhee wanted to stop.

"There's a grand place, Tim. Will we stay there, will we?" Overwhelmed by the suddenness of the idea, Mr. McPhee stared at the door, reluctant to make a move. I suggested, perhaps with insensitive American directness, that we ask if there were any vacancies. Mr. McPhee demurred with mysteriously excessive sensitivity, looking at me as if I had suggested we do something highly illegal.

"Should we inquire, de ye think?"

"I think we should. It's the only way we'll find out if they have any room." He thought about that for a moment, still very unsure.

"Will I go inside and ask, then?" He seemed almost frightened.

"Or I could, if you like."

"Ye would?"

Michael Garvey

The McPhees waited in the car while I nego-
tiated for a double and a single. When I returned with the lodging arrangements complete, Mr. McPhee looked at me with open admiration, and Molly said that I'd been lovely
about the whole thing. I really felt that I'd accomplished something.

"Ye seem to be a lad that's traveled," said
Timothy McPhee.

I left the McPhees to settle into their quar-
ters, and, warmed by the afterglow of my
triumphant success in fearlessly procurring
our rooms, approached the landlady to find out
about a bath. She seemed doubtful, her expression and tone implying that the taking of a
bath was a very serious step for a man of my
age and background. "There *is* a bath, of
course, on the third floor, but we'll need
another 25p, and we ask that ye be quite
sparing with the water."

It may be true, as some of my Irish friends
have suggested, that Americans have a clean-
liness fetish, that there is something unnatur-
al, perhaps perverse about our habits of daily
bathing; but that is perhaps the sole American
trait that I would absolutely refuse to relin-
quish. After three days without a bath, you
begin to itch and the world seems a hostile,
alien place. I paid the 25p, apologized for the

inconvenience, and was not at all sparing with the water.

Bundoran was as mixed up as a dog's breakfast, combining elements of a charming fishing village, a garish Reno, Nevada gambling complex, and an elegant seaside resort. Slot machines and pinball games proliferated, and the incongruous Jamaican reggae music of Bob Marely and the Wailers boomed out of the record&tape shops; songs about tropical sun, potent cannabis, sexual license, and general riot echoing in the grey, damp streets. I might have been dreaming.

In a diner close to the Bed and Breakfast place, uneasily caught in a weird vortex of urinous yellow lights and chiming pinballs, I decided to try the meal most common to inexpensive Irish menus: Beans on Toast. When the waitress came to take my order, I tried to be casual, not quite believing that people really ate beans on toast, afraid that it might be a humorous trap for the timid visitor tempted to ingratiate himself by imitation of local custom. I was astounded when she returned to the table with my order. The menu had been painstakingly accurate; on the plate before me were two pieces of toast, smothered with baked beans, and the waitress' face was impassive as a poker player's. For all I know, the concept of beans on toast may really be a joke; I saw it advertised everywhere in Ireland, but I never say anyone eat it. Pretending that it was a common American dish, I thanked the waitress, asked for pepper, and ate.

At the table next to mine, four thin, severe looking old women chatted happily about one of their contemporaries. The woman had, apparently, undergone exploratory surgery which had revealed an inoperable cancer, and there was something savage and gleeful about their noisy compassion.

"Dear, sweet Jesus, the poor woman."

"And her not knowing a thing about it."

"Does she not?"

"They've only found out yesterday."

"Did they tell Joseph?"

"They did not."

"And will he come when he knows?"

"He will, surely."

"Did they tell Bride?"

"They did, of course."

"And what did she say, poor thing?"

"She *won't* be comforted."

"And when did Bride hear of it?"

And on and on and on. Never had I heard such unbounded pleasure in tragedy expressed since the Dominican nuns in my grade school told us about what the Red Chinese

Communists had done to the missionaries. I left the diner with half a dozen baked beans uneaten on my plate, the pinballs ringing in the yellow light, and the spinsters keening over the imminent death of their friend.

That love of suffering; where did it come from? Some people in Ireland will tell you that it is a legacy of Cornelius Jansen. Others will tell you that it is a permanent characteristic of Celtic genes, subsisting in the conscience of the race. I remember reading someplace that during the barbarian invasions, the Celts had an opportunity to sack Rome. Surrounding the city, hordes of naked men and women, their bodies painted blue and their hair powdered white held Rome in terror for days. Their battle cries, incoherent to the Roman ear, echoed ominously through the suburban streets until the Romans offered them a large ransom if they would agree to leave. The ransom was accepted and Rome was left financially depleted, but physically intact.

The reason, I'm sure, is this: the barbarian Celts, with Rome's jugular vulnerable and exposed, immediately divided into two camps when ransom was proposed. One camp insisted that Rome be sacked, the other, that the ransom be accepted and that they all go home to celebrate. Verbal quarrels led soon to fistfights to bloodshed. Remorse, guilt, and communal suffering led to weeping, commiseration and Byzantine evaluations of tribal disunity. From the coffers of the astounded Romans, the saddened barbarians accepted a fortune in gold and vanished, weeping and confused, into the obscurity of ancient history. That explanation may be completely worthless but it seemed that night, with the memory of the spinsters' conversation so recent, more plausible than any other.

The traditional Irish music featured at one bar in Bundoran had been recommended to me by Irish friends, and I penetrated the haze of neon and reggae to find it.

The large window which fronted the street displayed a gigantic poster: SMASH H BLOCK. Ulster was too close to be forgotten here. Inside the place, I found the only jukebox I've ever seen in Ireland, riveted to the bar and blaring Republican songs. The bar surface was strewn with empty pint glasses and collection boxes, for the Foreign Missions, for the Lifeboats, for the Vincent De Paul Society, for the Sinn Fein Party, for the Relatives Action Committee. And there were stacks and stacks of leaflets proposing Irish unification, British withdrawal, a Socialist Parliamentary System and the immediate release of political prisoners.

The jukebox was playing a song called "My Little Armalite," a jaunty ode to the automatic weapon preferred by the Provisional I.R.A. and sung so cheerfully that it might have been a comic love story. Deeper in the building there was a large dancehall, empty except for a small group of musicians halfheartedly arranging their instruments and sound equipment on a plywood stage.

The ode to the Armalite Rifle had finished, and the band seemed slow in its preparations; I ordered a Guinness and brought it to the jukebox for a browse. The selections were entirely concerned with the history of Irish disunity from 1916 to the present, and, for the most part, entirely new to me. Finally, I was able to choose the number "Crossmaglen." An exuberant tune carried by an engaging rhythm, "Crossmaglen" is emblematic of the strangeness of the Ulster tragedy, describing the rural South Armagh town more bloodied and wartorn than any other in the country. But the bright tune and complex harmony closely resemble "Hello, Mary Lou," by the Everly Brothers. As is the case with so many Irish rebel songs, there is an odd combination of sincere patriotism and lusty singsong, and the listener happily taps his foot to descriptions of death, devastation and shattered hopes.

Still slightly stunned by the incongruity, I

discovered that I'd struck up a conversation with a building inspector from Donegal town. How this came about I'm not sure, as the man was quiet, mildly depressed and disinclined to talk. After one long silence he asked (what else?), "American, are ye?"

"No, Portugese." He looked blankly at me, and I felt more like an idiot than before.

"I don't like Americans much." The building inspector was a large man, and he had two untouched pints of Guinness before him in addition to the one which he had drained between my joke about being Portugese and his observation of his feelings toward folks of my background and accent. His eyes were bloodshot, and his quiet demeanor reminded me of the rugby players at Notre Dame, who wore sweatshirts with the legend, "Rugby Players Eat Their Dead." I had just made a tired and smartassed joke, he was in the early, volatile stages of intoxication, and had uttered the last sentence with the nonchalance of a Mafia don ordering a hit. The door of the bar was roughly fifteen feet away, and I couldn't remember if it opened into the bar or out to the street; there was no furniture between my place at the bar and the door; if I left the stool in my wake, it could trip him up, giving me almost thirty feet of advantage, but possibly making him angrier than before . . . I made myself stop thinking that way, and struggled to keep any betrayal of panic out of my pinched voice.

"Oh?" Why is that?" He stared for a while at his next pint before he spoke. I thought about lighting a cigarette, but was afraid my hands would tremble.

"It has never," the building inspector said patiently, "been satisfactorily explained to myself or to anyone with whom I'm acquainted, why America went so quickly to Britain's aid during the Second World War."

I relaxed slightly. That, after all, had not been my generation, and there as something (perhaps unjustifiably) reassuring about the intricacy of his grammar. Surely articulate Donegal building inspectors posed no physical threat to innocent American tourists, and surely the emotional reactions of a man so careful to avoid a terminal preposition would be restrained by a rational analysis of the situation. He was, nevertheless, getting drunk.

"Oh, that. Well, the Japanese attack on Pearl Harbor . . . "

"That explains only Roosevelt's declaration of war on Japan, *not* the alliance with the Brits." This guy was serious.

"Well, what about the Nazis, then? There were the deathcamps, the . . . "

Michael Garvey

"I am not at all defending Naziism. Neither was De Valera when he insisted upon neutrality." Tears welled in the building inspector's eyes and his voice became choked; he began to quote De Valera's famous response to Churchill's charge of Irish compliance: "Could he not find the generosity in his heart" to see that there was one small nation that also stood alone, not for one year, but for hundreds against a foreign threat . . . He wiped his eyes and became challenging again. "Naziism had nothing to do with it, I tell you."

"Well, then, what about the deathcamps?"

"You didn't know about the deathcamps then. None of us did. That's mere tergiversation." I was stunned, not only by the man's stubborn opposition to the American-Britain alliance, but by the fact that he could so casually drop into a conversation a word I had never heard uttered before. It was a week later that I found a dictionary to look it up.

I continued to tergiversate, but finally agreed with the man that the alliance had never been satisfactorily explained to us, either. That seemed to satisfy him, and he continued to drink and to quote De Valera's defense of Irish neutrality and to weep and to drink more until I myself felt safely neutral.

Not only had he seemed to forget my nationality, he had become oblivious to my presence at the bar as well.

The place had begun to fill with locals, Irish tourists, German college students, and a busload of Americans, noisy and embarrassing as caricatures. The volume of chatter was high, the jukebox had been disconnected, and the band was beginning to tune up.

A smiling, overweight, balding Chicagoan was suddenly bellowing a long, complicated order at the sullen barman. He had told everyone from the crowd around the doorway to the bar that he was from Chicago, that his name was O'Brien, that he could drink with the best of them and God only knows what else. His trousers were flaming red, his shoes were snow white, and garish shamrocks festooned the back of his golden ski jacket. The short "a's" in his speech were so flattened that O'Brien required two syllables to pronounce "Bass," the brand of ale which slopped liberally on the countertop as he gestured with his glass at the fortunately comatose form of the building inspector. "What's wich yer pal, there? Gotta little blasted, looks like."

"Yeah, I guess he did." I regretted instantly the length of my response and the consequent revelation of my nationality. Already deep scarlet, the face of the Chicagoan became twice inflamed.

"Holy Christ almighty!" O'Brien was roaring and exhilarated, "Yer American! I'll be goddamed! Hey! Marge! Eddie! This guy here's from America! Looks as Irish as a goddamn leprechaun, don't he? I'll just be god*damned!*" Needless to say, this encounter of fellow expatriates attracted the immediate and not entirely sympathetic attention of everyone in the place, and as Marge and Eddie rushed through the crowd to confirm O'Brien's observation, I began to envy the unconsciousness of the Donegal patriot.

Miserable, I coenthused with Marge and Eddie about Guinness, greenery, local charm and blue eyes while O'Brien kneaded my left shoulder with demonstrative affection.

"I just love it over here," he explained to me and to everyone else in the bar. "They're all so friendly. I was over here last year, ya know, and they didn't have any ice on the goddamn island, I swear to God. But that's one thing we taught 'em, for sure. We taught 'em how to make ice, didn't we. Huh? Didn't we, pal?" His last remarks, although loud enough to be heard throughout Bundoran, were particularly addressed to the barman, who smiled icily at all of us and agreed in an exaggerated brogue.

"Oh, ye did, surely. We've mountains of ice, now." I began to wish I were in Sweden, and I suspect that the barman wished we all were. Mercifully, the band struck up a loud version of "James Connolly, the Irish Rebel" and the further, more detailed observations of Mr. O'Brien were drowned in the chorus.

The Music temporarily roused the building inspector, upon whom O'Brien descended like a falcon; tactfully, the barman distracted the man from Chicago with an imaginative, spontaneous recipe for Irish coffee until the man from Donegal had again fallen asleep. Everyone sang rebel songs.

Later that evening, the McPhees reappeared, shyly agreeing, after much reassurance, to sit with O'Brien, Marge, Eddie, and myself. Molly and Marge, both slightly tipsy, discussed the reasons for Jacqueline Kennedy's marriage to Aristotle Onassis. O'Brien, very drunk, lectured Mr. McPhee, Eddie and me about the charms of Ireland. Timothy McPhee, expressionless and sipping white lemonade, told me later that evening (I believe, in all sincerity) that he couldn't remember having had a more pleasant holiday. "That O'Brien's fierce witty," said Timothy McPhee.

"Ye Yanks are great ones for the crack."

So much had the McPhees enjoyed the evening, they decided in the morning to spend another day at Bundoran. Molly McPhee and Marge O'Brien were going together to the hairdresser's, and O'Brien, Eddie, and Timothy McPhee were going to find a golf course. At breakfast, I met an Australian couple who offered me a ride further North.

State O'Chassis

*E*VEN if this story does not, as I suspect, speak for itself, I am unable to formulate an appropriate comment:

There was a man standing in the square of Donegal town (and he is probably standing in that spot right now) who told me that I must not fail to see Killybegs, where he was born.

"When the darkness falls and the moonlight strikes the water round the boats, ye will never see a thing like it anywhere else. Ye become so sad it's delightful."

Another: In a bar in Dingle, I saw two men fall into a ferocious quarrel about which mountain, Brandon or Carrauntoohil, was Ireland's highest. The argument was brought to an abrupt halt by the intervention of a gigantic pro-Brandon man. His voice trembled with anger as he spoke to the dissenter, "Don't degrade my favorite mountain!"

And another: In Clare, a woman gave me a lift from the driveway of her house to Kinvarra, in Galway. Making small talk, I asked her how far it was from her house to Kinvarra, and she replied: "It always used to be fifteen miles."

And another: I asked my Dublin landlady how far her house was from the Dublin airport. "That depends," she said. Nothing more.

Michael Garvey

"It is the presence of man that renders natural existence interesting."

Denis Diderot,
Encyclopedia

I SIT in a drab green room in Iowa, listening to the monotonous whine of synthetic rubber tires on the wet street outside. Fun.

Off the Kerry headlands, mountainous waves are smashing against the rocks of the outlying islands, sending jets of white spray hundreds of feet into the evening air, and the seagulls are shrieking with the same frenzy. All this has been going on since long before the days of Brendan the Navigator and will go on and on, long after we've finished scarring and plundering the planet. The saxifrage of the weird lunar surface of Clare's Burren country is still doing its slow, deleterious work, trying to push the great rocks further apart to admit light and air to the old earth below, and in the mountains of Donegal, a fine rain is unsuccessfully attempting to penetrate the thick, thatched cottage roofs. Puffins, contemplative and loony, are perched along the lush banks of the Kenmare River staring at other puffins on the scattered river islands. Along the Shannon, corncrakes are yelling at each other through the hay; cloudshadows are floating across the ripening fields. And I mustn't forget the "bee-loud vales".

Few lands are as beautiful as Ireland; nobody disputes that. A dark amalgam of powerful forces from the British Empire to the modern multinational corporations is, of course, a continuing threat to the natural splendor of the island. Despite a large and variegated antinuclear movement, for instance, there will probably soon be a large nuclear power plant in Carnsore, Wexford; oil discovery threatens miles of previously unblemished shoreline; Ford Motors has arrived in Cork, and God only knows what delights the European Economic Community has planned for the remainder of the millenium.

During the few years which elapsed between my last visit to Ireland and this one, the island had become a much different place, and there is no reason to believe that in another decade it will not have become even more strange. The change disturbs me, but I have no rights in the matter. I don't live there, and my future depends little on the historical and cultural earthquake which seems to be in store. In Dublin, I heard an exasperated bricklayer explain the situation to another "Yank with all the answers" as we sat with our pints in the

Wexford Inn: "Ye've a right lot of advice and tunes, but I don't remember anyone draggin' ye here fer yer wisdom. If ye've done such a bloody fine job in America, ye're entitled to stay there as long as ye like!"

But I thought, as the annoyed bricklayer so understandably silenced the condescending American, that it wasn't the oceans and mountains and landscapes and quaint villages which drew us to the island each year in such great numbers. It was to hear exactly that sort of judgment pronounced in a gritty Dublin accent, an accent which seemed designed for irony and storytelling. Or it was to meet with people whose sadness and frustration reverberated with our own; to meet plumbers who possessed a scholar's knowledge of the Huguenot struggles, and traffic cops as articulate as ambassadors.

If there is such a reality as "the Irish character" (and to try to gather into a cohesive idea the millions of its aspects would give anyone a spiritual hernia), it is that which makes the island fascinating. If the inhabitants and customs and manners and tastes of that small island could be moved intact to the Oklahoma panhandle, even that desolate stretch of our continent would attract curious visitors by the thousands. And in Ireland, which must be the most literate and emotionally sensitive country in the world, everyone is aware of this. That very awareness gives to every encounter between visitor and native a self-consciousness which only deepens the mystery and quickens the attraction. It will forever remain to be seen whether that puzzling phenomenon is a fortune or a tragedy. In any event, the Irish will never be left alone.